IMAGES
of America

PALM BEACH COUNTY DURING WORLD WAR II

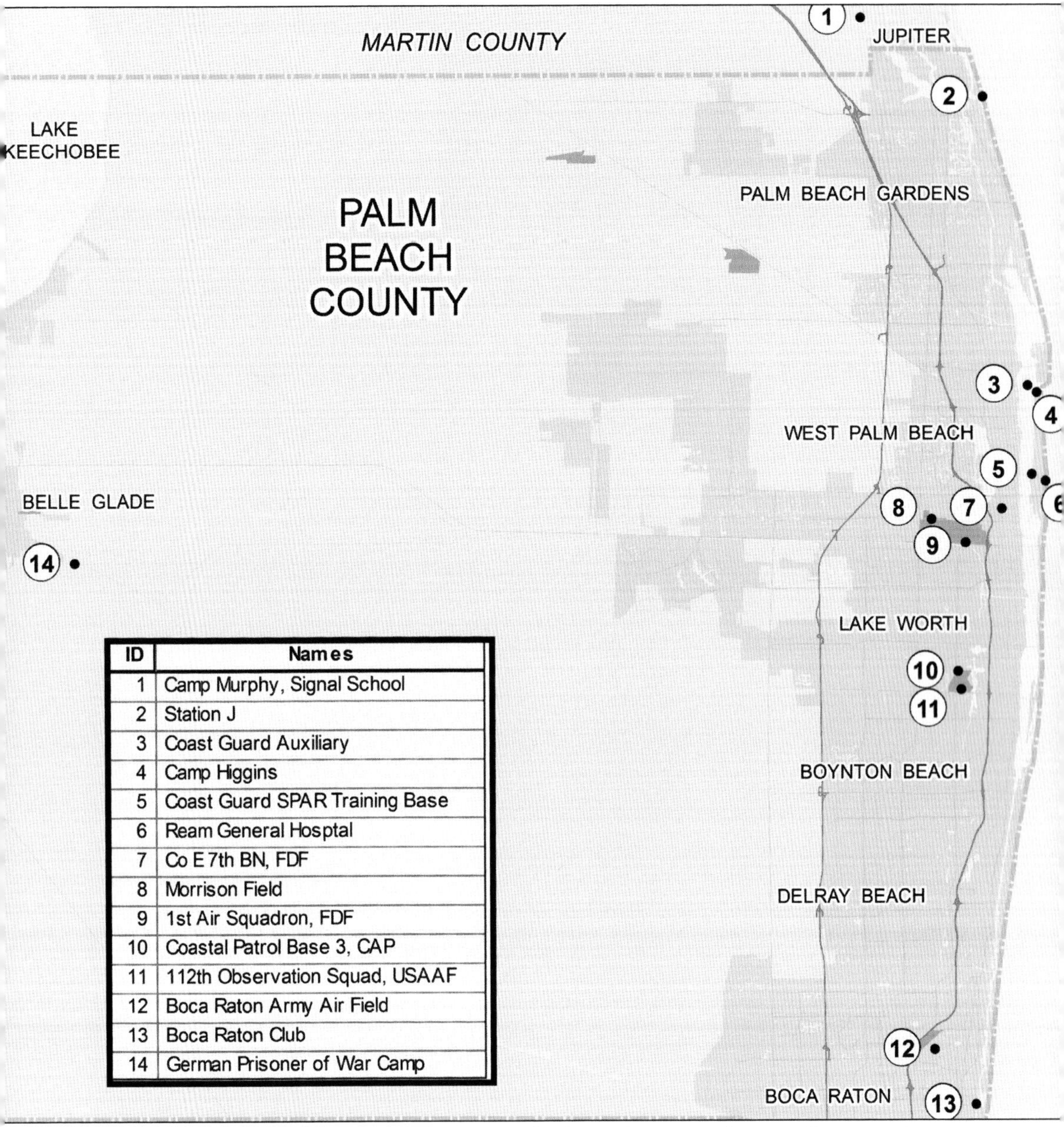

ID	Names
1	Camp Murphy, Signal School
2	Station J
3	Coast Guard Auxiliary
4	Camp Higgins
5	Coast Guard SPAR Training Base
6	Ream General Hosptal
7	Co E 7th BN, FDF
8	Morrison Field
9	1st Air Squadron, FDF
10	Coastal Patrol Base 3, CAP
11	112th Observation Squad, USAAF
12	Boca Raton Army Air Field
13	Boca Raton Club
14	German Prisoner of War Camp

During World War II, Palm Beach County was a beehive of activity. The map illustrates the various locations of the different military and volunteer bases in the county, including a prisoner-of-war camp in Belle Glade. All the branches of military served in the county. (Richard Randall.)

On the Cover: In May 1943, the Boca Raton Army Air Field received its first group of Women's Army Auxiliary Corps (WAACs), which became the Women's Army Corps (WACs) in July 1943. These women served in a wide variety of base support functions. WAC uniforms were notoriously ill-fitting and uncomfortable in the Florida climate. These WACs do not seemed pleased to be suffering through yet another inspection. (Boca Raton Historical Society & Museum.)

IMAGES
of America

PALM BEACH COUNTY DURING WORLD WAR II

Susan Gillis, Richard A. Marconi,
and Debi Murray

ARCADIA
PUBLISHING

Copyright © 2015 by Susan Gillis, Richard A. Marconi, and Debi Murray
ISBN 978-1-4671-1401-1

Published by Arcadia Publishing
Charleston, South Carolina

Printed in the United States of America

Library of Congress Control Number: 2014959794

For all general information, please contact Arcadia Publishing:
Telephone 843-853-2070
Fax 843-853-0044
E-mail sales@arcadiapublishing.com
For customer service and orders:
Toll-Free 1-888-313-2665

Visit us on the Internet at www.arcadiapublishing.com

This book is dedicated to the men and women who served our country during World War II. Without their sacrifice, the world would not be free.

Contents

Acknowledgments

We would like to thank Maggie Bullwinkel for her encouragement during the writing of this book and the Historical Society of Palm Beach County (HSPBC), the Boca Raton Historical Society & Museum (BRHSM), the US Air Force Historical Research Agency (USAFHRA), and the Florida State Archives (FSA) for the use of their extensive collections of photographs and research material. Without it, this book would not have been possible.

For the information on the Boca Raton Army Air Field and Boca Raton during World War II, we would like to express our sincere thanks to Sally Ling for her book *Small Town, Big Secrets* (2005). This book would not have been possible without her extensive research and information about the minute details of everyday life at BRAAF. The information gathered for her book is now available in the collections of the Boca Raton Historical Society & Museum. The following represent the veterans and civilians whose photographs and memories have made this book possible: Jim Barnt, Martha and Peter Barrett, Richard H. Becker, Charlie Bender, Stan Biedron, Archie and Irene Carswell, Manny Chavez, William Coburn Clark, Louis Delgado, Eldra Durham, Frank Fisher Jr., Phil Kantor, Edith Mize Lewis, Harry Magafan, Anne Maguire, Ed Malavarca, Orlo Maxfield, James McCrudden, Bill Murden, Waino Ray, Paul Schweisburg, Charles Winslow Skeele, and Alvin Thiele.

Introduction

Fearing attack on the mainland after the devastation at Pearl Harbor, Hawaii, civilians and military personnel alike prepared to defend their country. The threat of invasion from both Japan and Germany seemed very real. Florida residents could hear explosions and see evidence of the danger lurking just offshore, when Allied ships were left drifting, ablaze and sinking, their crews awaiting rescue or dying after attacks by U-boats.

Nearly everyone in the United States, from children to those long past retirement, participated in some way to help defeat Germany, Japan, and Italy during World War II. Children helped collect scrap materials. Adults and teenagers volunteered for civil defense, manning coastal watchtowers or acting as blackout wardens. American Red Cross volunteers taught first-aid courses, rolled bandages, and otherwise prepared for invasion by Germany. Men and women enlisted in the military in numbers never seen before. New military bases and even a prisoner-of-war camp were built in Palm Beach County. War was no longer something happening far away—war was at the doorstep.

During World War II, Palm Beach County was an integral cog in the war machine established by the Allies against the Axis powers. From Jupiter to Boca Raton, various branches of the military operated numerous facilities—from convalescent hospitals to training centers and spying on German communications. Palm Beach County was a dynamic and vibrant hub of military activity. The first of these, and the longest-lasting, was Morrison Field Army Air Base, located at what is now Palm Beach International Airport.

For 17 months, a group of volunteers serving in the Civil Air Patrol helped fight one of the biggest threats to our country's safety: German submarines called U-boats. They hunted their prey along the East Coast of the United States and in the Gulf of Mexico. Men and women of the Civil Air Patrol volunteered their time and resources to help protect our shores from the U-boat menace.

The US Army began construction of Boca Raton Army Air Field on 5,820 acres in south Palm Beach County in May 1942. Of the 831 buildings on the base by August 1943, there were 11 mess halls, 3 chapels, 50 recreation buildings, 6 hangers, 335 enlisted barracks, 20 officer barracks, 16 school buildings, and 9 stores. As many as 100,000 servicemen and women trained or worked at the field before it closed in 1947.

When regular Coast Guardsmen were assigned to war duties overseas, volunteers once again stepped into the breach. Members of Coast Guard Temporary Reserves Flotilla 3, Division 2, were proud to call themselves members of the "Hooligan Navy." The men used their own boats, usually unarmed, to assume the duties the Coast Guard typically performed. Since boat traffic in general was curtailed, they did not have to rescue many day sailors or fishermen, but they played a vital role in rescuing merchant marine crewmen from torpedoed ships. The women's component of the Coast Guard converted the Biltmore Hotel into a training base for enlisted personnel.

The Palm Beach County Chapter of the American Red Cross also relied on volunteers to work at the military bases, training centers, railroad stations, and hospitals around Palm Beach County, where they manned canteens, helped patients, and provided assistance to the troops. With gas rationing leaving many families without transportation, the motor corps drove other volunteers to their posts, transported civilians to medical appointments, and took convalescing servicemen and women on outings. They supplied survivors from merchant ships attacked by U-boats with medical care, clothing, food, lodging, and transportation home. In every goal set by the National American Red Cross for individual chapters, from people trained in first aid to fundraising, Palm Beach County exceeded its quota.

World War II was the last war to affect all aspects of American life. The government instituted rationing of gasoline, manufactured goods, and food, especially sugar and coffee. Civilians collected newspapers, aluminum, rubber, and even bacon grease for the war effort. Blackouts and air raid warnings became regular occurrences.

After V-E Day, focus at the local airfields switched to the Pacific; Morrison Field had plans extending through July 1946 to prepare planes and crews for the push against Japan. V-J Day and the end of the war changed everything. The military and civilians alike began the process of welcoming returning soldiers. Trainloads of soldiers traveled north from Miami, stopping at various stations along the way, including West Palm Beach. Service clubs, including the Jaycees, American Red Cross, Woman's Club, and Scouting organizations met each train, passing out goodies such as watermelon and soft drinks to the homebound servicemen.

The war changed Florida forever in a myriad of ways. The government abandoned land no longer necessary militarily, either selling it or giving it to the state, which in turn found new uses for the properties. Camp Murphy became Jonathan Dickinson State Park, part of Boca Raton Army Air Field reverted to a private airport, and some of the runways became the site of Florida Atlantic University in 1961. Other parts of Boca Raton became housing developments. Morrison Field returned to Palm Beach County, which expanded the facilities for public use. The airfield returned to government control as Palm Beach Air Force Base during the Korean War and remained so until 1959, the end of the original 20-year lease.

Many soldiers remembered their wartime stays in Florida fondly, and thousands returned to the state after the war to raise their families, kicking off a building boom that lasted until the Great Recession of the early 21st century. Other soldiers vacationed in Florida for decades, and they and others retired to the state where they took up new jobs or hobbies such as golf, fishing, and hosting other family members for their vacations. The retirees are also great volunteers—giving time and service to untold numbers of nonprofit organizations that enrich the lives of the more than 1.3 million people currently living in Palm Beach County.

One

Morrison Army Air Field

In 1940, Palm Beach County leased its airport for 20 years to the US government for an Army air base for $1 per annum. Lengthening of runways and construction of buildings along Belvedere Road began that November, and in February 1941, the Third Army Air Force's 8th Wing Headquarters moved into its new quarters with the 49th Pursuit Group and 51st Air Base Group arriving shortly afterward. The primary purpose of the base was fighter pilot training and monitoring the U-boats patrolling offshore. After December 7, 1941, mechanics crated the planes, and both planes and crews shipped out the first week in January: the 49th Pursuit Group to the Pacific and the 51st Air Base Group to the Indochina and the Africa–Middle East theaters.

By the end of January, Morrison Field became the center of Project X, designed to furnish embattled American forces in the Philippines with 65 bombers, which was so successful, the Air Transport Command chose the base as an aerial port of embarkation—the last US soil American crews would see before entering combat.

More than 15,000 planes and their crews were processed through the base on their way to battle before the end of the war. Airplanes received final checks and repairs; men received physicals, shots, and appropriate uniforms and wrote wills and final letters home, including their "in case I don't make it back" letters. The aircrews were restricted to the base in an attempt to keep troop movements secret.

The end of hostilities in August 1945 lessened the demands on Morrison Field, and the Army Air Corps closed the base on June 30, 1947. The US Air Force reopened the field as Palm Beach Air Force Base in 1951 in response to the start of hostilities in Korea. Although the Air Force wanted to make the base a permanent installation, Palm Beach County officials thought a modern international airport was more beneficial to the area, and Palm Beach Air Force Base closed for the last time in 1959.

After months of intense negotiations, Palm Beach County commissioner Cecil "Zeke" Cornelius (1902–1976) enticed the US government to lease Morrison Field for military use. Using local contractors and workers, the Work Projects Administration (WPA) enlarged Morrison Field's runways and constructed numerous airplane hangars, barracks, and administration buildings, turning the majority of the county's airport into an Army air field. Zeke owned Cornelius Insurance Agency and, in his spare time, volunteered as a pilot in the First Air Squadron, Florida Defense Force, transferring to the Civil Air Patrol when activated in March 1942. Commissioned as a second lieutenant in the Army Air Forces in July 1943, he was stationed at Morrison Field, where he helped brief transient airplane crews about the hazards of the route they were about to follow on their way to war. After the war, Zeke returned to his insurance company, which he expanded, adding partners Richard S. Johnson and William C. Clark, forming Cornelius, Johnson, and Clark, the county's largest independent insurance agency. (HSPBC.)

Local companies were sourced as contractors, including Watt and Sinclair of Florida, Inc. and Cleary Brothers Construction, who were happy to have the job after years with few building projects. The total price for construction was $2,417,651. Morrison Field was officially accepted and assigned to the Third Air Force as an Army installation on February 27, 1941, when Lt. Col. John W. Monahan assumed command. (USAFHRA.)

Visiting aircraft included the "faintin' floozie III," an F-8-DH Mosquito, a photographic reconnaissance aircraft flown by Lt. Col. Karl "Pops" Polifka (second from right), who earned the Distinguished Service Cross in 1943 for service during an aerial reconnaissance mission over Mount Maggiori, Italy. Polifka earned the Silver Star Medal posthumously for his gallantry in action during the Korean War in 1951. (HSPBC.)

At first, only a few Air Corps trained officers were assigned to the base. Instead, reserve officers from different branches—including Artillery, Coast Artillery, Infantry, and the National Guard—were stationed there. By the end of March, Detachment 245th Separate Quartermaster Company had reported to the base. Included in the company were the first African Americans assigned there. The primary mission of Morrison Field was to train fighter and pursuit pilots, and toward this end, the 8th Pursuit Wing and the 49th Pursuit Squadron, which included P-35s and P-40s, arrived at Morrison Field. Flying east over Morrison Field, the P-35 pilots pictured had an uninterrupted view of the emptiness of the land west of the city of West Palm Beach. To the north, they could see the horse track formerly owned by Murray D. Carmichael and the nearly empty subdivision of Westgate. (USAFHRA.)

Construction continued on Morrison Field throughout 1941, including a 600,000-gallon fuel tank to refuel heavy bombers flying to Caribbean areas and a hospital with attendant medical facilities. Most of the buildings were one- and two-story structures with lots of windows to catch every breeze. Since the military was still segregated, duplicate facilities were required for black and white troops. For the most part, African American soldiers worked as mechanics and drivers for the base's motor corps, cooks, and clerks. They had separate barracks, mess halls, recreation facilities, and post exchanges (stores). (Both, USAFHRA.)

On December 7, 1941, all Army personnel, except married officers, were restricted to base, and the guard at the gates trebled. Lieutenant Colonel Monahan ordered a complete blackout. On Christmas Day, the 49th and 51st Groups were alerted for immediate overseas service. Crewmen spent the next 10 days knocking down their planes and crating them for shipment. Both groups left Morrison Field on January 3, 1942. The 49th was sent to the southwest Pacific, some to Java and the rest to Australia. The 51st went to Africa and India where they were later assigned to the Air Transport Command and formed the nucleus for the India-China Wing and the Africa–Middle East Wing. The total enlisted strength at Morrison Field went from 2,060 men to 200, leaving a very large gap in the defense of Palm Beach County. (Both, HSPBC.)

No longer was Morrison Field a training base; by the end of January, it was transferred to the Air Corps Ferrying Command, which in turn became the Air Transport Command (ATC). Under the guidance of a new commanding officer, Col. Paul E. Burrows (above), Morrison became the leading winter port of embarkation for all major war fronts. The first effort to supply troops on the ground was titled Project X, which furnished embattled American forces in the Philippines with 65 bombers, both Liberators and Fortresses (B-17s and B-24s). The operation was so successful that it came to the attention of the higher-ups in Washington, who decided to retain Morrison in the ferrying command. At the same time, all civilian aircraft except for the Civil Air Patrol and Eastern Airlines were banned from the field. (Both, USAFHRA.)

Throughout 1942, Morrison Field continued to grow. Construction of new hangars took precedence, as the space was vital for servicing airplanes for overseas duty. The base soon boasted a variety of schools, including finance, medical officers' basic training, and ordnance. Eventually, all ATC ordnance personnel graduated from the Morrison school. Included in this roster was an airborne radar school (one of the first in the country), which opened in March and was the forerunner of the radar school at Boca Raton Army Air Base. Approximately 300 men graduated per month, until the school moved to Boca in late July 1942. (Above, USAFHRA; below, HSPBC.)

In the eight months leading up to the invasion of France (October 1943–May 1944), Morrison Field processed 6,216 planes and 45,344 flying personnel, despite a reduction in enlisted men. The first WAC detachment of just over 200 women arrived on May 3, 1944, which replaced men in transportation and administrative assignments, freeing them for overseas duty. At the same time, the Air Corps started an operational training program at the base, which qualified base personnel in the use of firearms (below) and chemical warfare. All base personnel, including the nurses at Morrison since 1942, were cross-trained, so when men were deployed to the fronts, the work could continue at Morrison without interruption or loss of productivity. Army nurse 2nd Lt. Emily M. Law (above), learning to drive cross-country in an Army jeep. (Both, HSPBC.)

Morrison Field became known as the Caribbean Wing of Air Transport Command and was the winter embarkation point for the Army Air Corps, especially when winter weather closed Northern facilities. Aircrews were sent to Morrison after leaving other training bases so men and aircraft could get final clearances for the long flights ahead. Supposedly, all travel destinations both in country and out were secret, but family members often arrived in town to find a complete lack of hotel space. Since crew members were restricted to base and only at Morrison a few days, families often missed seeing their soldier relatives. The men spent their days at Morrison checking their planes and equipment for needed repairs. They also got final medical clearance, any necessary inoculations, and dental work. (Above, HSPBC; below, USAFHRA.)

Air Transport Command was in charge of moving men, matériel, and equipment (including airplanes, ammunition, machine parts, and so forth) to battlefronts around the world. Pilots attended briefings detailing the routes they were to take through the Caribbean and beyond. If they flew out of the pattern called the Chennault Route (named for Claire Lee Chennault, who organized American Volunteer Group known as the Flying Tigers and planned the route to China over the Himalayas), they could be shot down by friendly fire, especially if they flew too close to Venezuela, where American ships guarded the oil fields. As the men rotated through their briefings, crews learned the importance of proper weight distribution on the aircraft and how to properly stow materials. (Both, USAFHRA.)

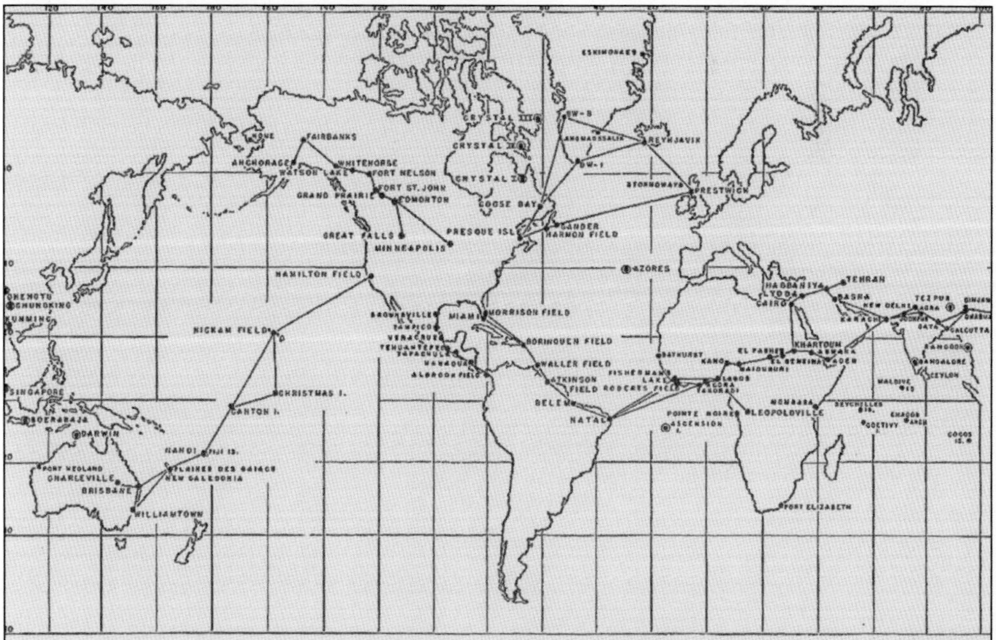

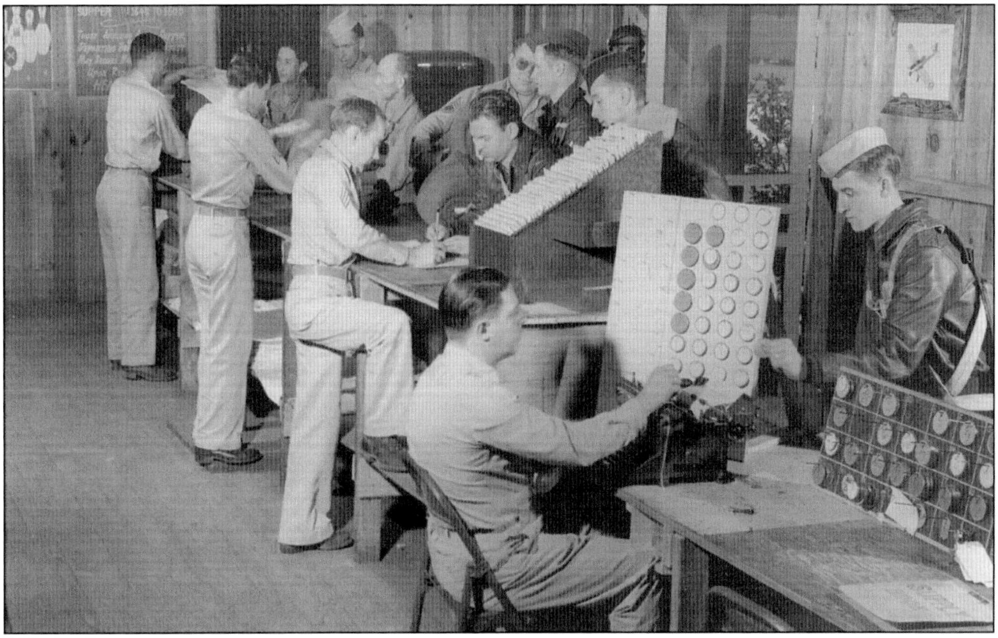

In crew briefings, the men discovered that not all the dangers ahead would come out of the barrels of enemy guns. The most constant perils were mosquitoes, food, water, and sexual relations, so they learned how to prevent tropical and venereal diseases. They also received jungle packs, aerosol bombs, medical kits, and appropriate uniforms for their destination. The airplanes, which were often brand-new and flying long-distance for the first time, were checked completely. Processing of planes and personnel usually took two days, during which time they were restricted to base in an attempt to limit the public's knowledge of how many planes and men were being sent overseas. The unarmed planes (no guns or ammunition in order to save on weight and conserve fuel) usually left between the hours of 1:00 and 4:00 a.m. (Both, USAFHRA.)

In May 1942, a food poisoning epidemic sickened 800 men after they ate spoiled ham in the mess hall, and more than 500 were hospitalized. The official history reports, "Enlisted men dropped to the streets of West Palm Beach and Palm Beach like flies two hours after the noon meal had been served at the base. They were brought to the field by . . . whatever conveyances could be marshaled." (HSPBC.)

A soldier stands guard as mechanics repair an A-26 attack bomber. Fears of invasion by parachutists and U-boat crews increased after December 7, 1941, and officials considered several options to protect Morrison Field, including gun emplacements on the perimeter. Increased foot and vehicle patrols, tanks, and 150-millimeter cannons at Camp Higgins at the north end of Palm Beach were used instead. (HSPBC.)

African American personnel of the 999th Quartermaster's Corps ensured that Morrison Field's complement of vehicles continued to operate, and more men arrived to fill the roles of those who had been posted to the various theaters of war. Most personnel turned out for the memorial service for Pres. Franklin Roosevelt on April 15, 1945. Despite the end of the war in Europe, Morrison Field continued to enlarge its facility in anticipation of returning war-weary planes and men and the need for ever more planes and men headed to the Pacific theater, for which there were plans in place through July 1946. Approximately 4,400 military personnel and 1,972 civilians worked at the field. (Above, HSPBC; below, USAFHRA.)

Two

Florida Defense Force and the Civil Air Patrol

Florida governor Spessard Holland stressed the importance of Florida's strategic position between the Atlantic Ocean and the Gulf of Mexico and that Florida must act to make defense preparations. After Florida's National Guard was called into active duty by the federal government, the state legislature passed the Florida Defense Act in April 1941. Under the act, a home guard of volunteers formed to fill the void left by the National Guard. The Florida Defense Force (FDF), under the command of the governor, included infantry and air units throughout the state that could respond to state emergencies.

Capt. Wright "Ike" Vermilya headed the 1st Air Squadron. In West Palm Beach, Morrison Field became the squadron headquarters, and the first 67 men and women mustered into service in May 1941. Aviators who enlisted brought their own aircraft, since the state did not provide them, to patrol Florida's coastline and perform other duties as required. Two months later, Company E, 7th Battalion, FDF, organized in West Palm Beach under the command of Richard D. Hill.

Just days before Pearl Harbor, on December 1, 1941, Fiorello H. La Guardia signed the order for the creation of the national Civil Air Patrol (CAP) under the Office of Civilian Defense. The CAP would be used by the Army Air Forces to hunt U-boats, which were attacking Allied shipping off the East and Gulf Coasts. One of the first bases, Coastal Patrol Base 3, organized at Morrison Field, absorbing the 1st Air Squadron, while the infantry units of the Florida Defense Force remained under state control.

Sworn into office 11 months before the attack on Pearl Harbor, Florida's wartime governor, Spessard L. Holland (1892–1971), worked with the state legislature to establish the State Defense Council to organize civil defenses for Florida, as the National Guard had been activated for federal service, leaving the state vulnerable. This home guard was an armed force equipped to handle internal state security matters and emergencies. Holland's military advisor Lt. Gen. Albert Blanding and state adjutant Brig. Gen. Vivian Collins took command of the FDF. Holland, a Florida native, earned the Distinguished Service Cross while serving in the 24th Aero Squadron during World War I. Afterward, he resumed his law career in Polk County, working as a prosecuting attorney and later a judge. In 1932, he became a state senator and served as such until his run for governor. During his term, Holland reformed the state's tax system, created the Florida Game and Fresh Water Commission, and petitioned the federal government for military bases. After the war, he became a US senator, a position he retained until his retirement in 1969. (FSA.)

Richard D. Hill (1900–1984), commissioned as a captain in the Florida Defense Force, commanded Palm Beach County's Company E, 7th Battalion, an infantry unit of the FDF. A senior executive with Florida Power and Light Company, he remained in the FDF until it was deactivated in 1947. Dick Hill Park, located on Clematis Street, was named in his honor, but the site was later turned into a parking lot. (HSPBC.)

The Army provided Enfield rifles (pictured) to the FDF but had to recall the weapons once the United States entered the war. These were replaced by 12-gauge shotguns, .45-caliber submachine guns, and gas hand grenades. The state provided grey uniforms, which were later changed to khaki. The company practiced drills and ceremonial procedures at Wright Field Baseball Park in West Palm Beach. (HSPBC.)

Company E, 7th Battalion, FDF, stands in formation at the National Guard armory, now the Armory Arts Center, in West Palm Beach. It was the home of the activated Company C, 124th Infantry of the Florida National Guard. Capt. Richard D. Hill is standing on the left, at the head of the formation. The unit consisted of three officers and 62 enlisted men in two platoons, with three rifle squads each. (HSPBC.)

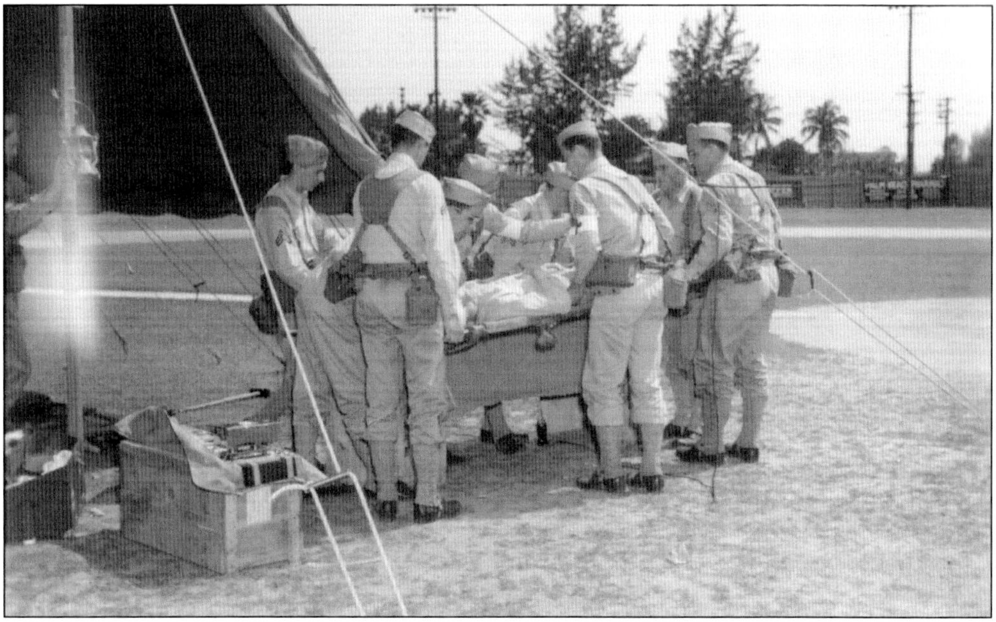

Members of Company E practice first aid on willing volunteers at Wright Field. The civilian volunteers had to undergo lots of training to be prepared for any situation, including hurricanes, tornadoes, riots, and attack by foreign powers. The baseball field became Connie Mack Field after the war in honor of Connie Mack, the owner and manager of the Philadelphia Athletics, who held spring training at the field. (HSPBC.)

In May 1941, the air arm of the FDF, the First Air Squadron, which enlisted men and women, mustered into service at Morrison Field. World War I aviator and president of Palm Beach Aero Corporation Wright Vermilya Jr. commanded the unit. Local businessmen and county officials such as Marshall E. Rinker Sr. and county commissioners John Prince and Cecil "Zeke" Cornelius volunteered with the unit. Some of the members are pictured in front of a Grumman G-21A Goose. A few of the identified members pictured here are Clarence "Cocky" Coston (first on the left), Art Keil (fourth from left), Wright Vermilya (seventh from left), Sally Coston (eighth from left), Wesley B. Jackson (fifth from right), and Zeke Cornelius (second from right). (HSPBC.)

Pictured here is the staff of the 1st Air Squadron in their headquarters at Morrison Field. Seated front center is Captain Vermilya and to his right is Zeke Cornelius, executive officer for the unit. Vermilya's staff included Ed Forbes (adjutant), Dr. H.A. Wakefield (flight surgeon), Jake Boyd (engineer), Thorne Donnelley (communications), Art Keil (photographer), John Prince (supply), Wally Maier (operations), and Roy Hime, Marshall E. Rinker, and Ted Keys (flight commanders). (HSPBC.)

A group of pilots of the First Air Squadron poses with some of the unit's planes, including Stinson Voyagers and a Grumman G-21A Goose (just inside the hanger) belonging to Palm Beach Aero Corporation. The squadron used the commercial hanger to service the airplanes. Capt. Ike Vermilya is on the left. (HSPBC.)

Members of the 1st Air Squadron stand inspection at their headquarters at Morrison Field. Aircrews stand next to their planes, most of which were Stinson Voyagers. The inspection team standing at attention on the left includes Captain Hill, commander of Company E, 7th Battalion, and Captain Vermilya, commander of the air squadron. (HSPBC.)

In January 1942, USAAF officers arrived in West Palm Beach to observe Florida's first air raid–spotter test, in which 15 aircraft from the 1st Air Squadron participated. These planes flew different routes over Palm Beach, Broward, and Dade Counties. When spotters heard or observed the airplanes, they called spotter headquarters. According to the military, the test was a success. (HSBPC.)

The 1st Air Squadron's collection of Stinson Voyagers is pictured here parked near the Palm Beach Aero Corporation's hangar and the small building that housed the squadron's headquarters in 1941. Palm Beach Aero was located on the Southern Boulevard side of the airport and provided fixed-base operations, servicing private airplanes with fuel and repairs. The Grumman Goose, parked the farthest west, an amphibious craft, also patrolled Florida's east coast searching for U-boats and was instrumental in recovering merchant sailors after their ships had been sunk by torpedoes. Southern Boulevard, to the left in the photograph, was still the only road to Belle Glade and other western communities. The vast emptiness to the west did not remain long once the Army Air Corps started servicing planes headed overseas. The Army's portion of the airport continued to expand through 1945. Some of the land was used for parking planes and as fuel and ammunition dumps. (HSPBC.)

In mid-December 1941, officials at the national Civil Air Patrol headquarters appointed Ike Vermilya the Civil Air Patrol Florida Wing commander. He was tasked with organizing state civilian aviation resources, which included surveying and documenting all private civilian aircraft and pilots. Vermilya was also instrumental in forming Florida's first CAP unit, Coastal Patrol Base 3, in response to Germany's launch of Operation Paukenschlag (Drumbeat) in early 1942. U-boat commanders had found merchant ships defenseless and took advantage of that once the United States declared war on Germany, all along the East and Gulf Coasts. Civilians could hear the explosive attacks on Allied ships, which occurred mostly at night, and as homeowners rose from their beds, they could see the ships burning offshore. By daylight, beachgoers were greeting by oil slicks, debris, and dead bodies on the beaches. (Right, HSPBC; below, LOC.)

To help combat U-boat attacks, the Army authorized the CAP to establish three experimental bases to perform antisubmarine patrols for Atlantic City, New Jersey, Rehoboth, Delaware, and West Palm Beach, Florida. The latter hosted Coastal Patrol Base 3. Florida's shipping lanes were the second-busiest in the United States and ranked sixth in the world. One out of every 12 ships sunk by U-boats was in Florida waters. (HSPBC.)

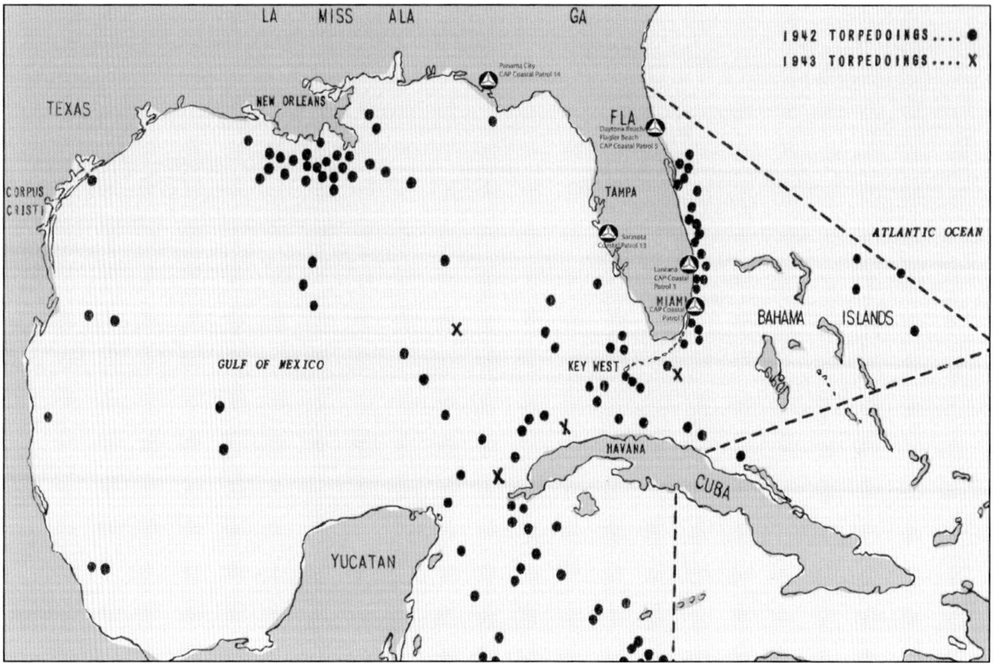

The CAP antisubmarine patrols were so successful in spotting U-boats, damaged and sinking ships, and survivors, that the national CAP soon established 18 more bases, stretching from Maine to Mexico. With five bases, West Palm Beach/Lantana, Flagler Beach, Miami, Sarasota, and Panama City, Florida, had the greatest number of facilities. (HSPBC.)

May 4, 1942, was a busy day for German submarine U-564. During daylight hours, the U-boat torpedoed the 9,400-ton British tanker *Eclipse* off of Boynton Beach, where beachgoers were frolicking in the waves. Two men were killed, and 45 reached shore in the ship's lifeboats. The ship was in shallow water and later towed to Fort Lauderdale for repairs. (HSPBC.)

Five miles off the Jupiter Inlet on May 4, 1942, at 11:00 p.m., a torpedo launched by U-564 struck the 35,000-ton US freighter *Delisle*, killing two crewmen. Survivors evacuated the crippled ship and were given aid by residents of Jupiter Island. The damaged vessel was repaired in Miami and returned to service. A year later, she struck a mine off Newfoundland and sank. (HSPBC.)

In 1942, an observer aboard a CAP plane took this photograph of a German submarine as it started its descent into the waters of the Atlantic Ocean. Submarines not only had to surface to recharge their batteries, they also surfaced to hunt merchantmen. The German captains did not know that the CAP planes were unarmed, and when they spotted the bright yellow machines, they dove for the bottom. After the war, a German captain's personal diary revealed that they were terrified of the little planes. If ships were salvageable after being attacked by a U-boat, they were towed to one of the repair facilities in Jacksonville, Fort Lauderdale, or Miami. (Both, HSPBC.)

Capt. Zack Mosley (1906–1993) poses beside his Stinson Reliant before an antisubmarine patrol around 1942. Mosley, an avid aviator and cartoonist from Stuart, Florida, created the syndicated *On the Wing* (later changed to *Smilin' Jack*) cartoon strip for the *Chicago Tribune* in 1933. Syndicated in over 300 newspapers, it ran until 1973 when Mosley retired. When Coastal Patrol 3 moved to Lantana Airfield, Mosley moved his art studio into a corner of the hanger so he could continue to work on his strip, using fellow pilots as inspiration for his characters. Mosley flew 300 hours during his time in the CAP and earned the military's Air Medal. In 1976, he was inducted into the US Air Force's Hall of Fame. He was the author of several books, including his autobiography, *Brave Coward Zack*. Mosley created the unit insignia, as seen over his right shoulder, after the aircraft were armed with bombs. The insignia was also used as the unit's patch. (HSPBC.)

During World War II, Zack Mosley continued to draw his *Smilin' Jack* comic strip. Smilin' Jack even joined the US Army Air Corps. Mosley also used his creative talents to draw unit insignia for the military and the Civil Air Patrol. As part of the CAP Public Relations section, he drew comic strips and posters about the roles of the CAP. In particular, Mosley drew upon his experiences with Coast Patrol Base 3 (CP3) and the mission of the coastal patrols who hunted the dreaded U-boats, as well as the other missions the volunteers performed. In this 1943 poster, Mosley briefly explains some of the history of the CAP, including the uniform and the fact that the CAP was transferred from the Office of Civilian Defense to the US War Department. (HSPBC.)

The barracuda bucket was a strange piece of survival equipment used by the aviators of coastal patrol units. Before the Army issued the civilian aviators small inflatable life rafts and "Mae West" life jackets, the airmen relied on a clumsy homemade device called a barracuda bucket, or bag. Sometimes called the "foxhole of the sea," it was a green canvas bag attached to a large inner tube and may have been an invention of Prohibition-era rumrunners. Stranded seamen used these bags to keep barracudas from taking a bite out of them. Coastal Patrol 3's communications officer Thorne Donnelly adapted the barracuda bag for use by the CAP in Florida. The bucket included a survival kit with a chocolate bar, mirror, flashlight, first-aid kit, water, and other survival items. (Both, HSPBC.)

While on patrol in May 1942, Marshall "Doc" Rinker and Tom Manning spotted a U-boat off Cape Canaveral. When the submarine tried to escape, it got stuck on a sandbar. The two men circled the stranded U-boat while radioing for the military. However, the U-boat freed itself and escaped. Gen. Hap Arnold heard about the incident and ordered all CAP planes on antisubmarine patrol to be armed with bombs or depth charges. Doc Rinker (1904–1996) moved from Indiana to Florida in 1925, the height of the building boom, and the following year he founded Rinker Materials Corporation, which he held until his retirement in 1988, when he sold the company to an Australian conglomerate. He and his family then founded several foundations that support the endeavors of institutions of higher learning, including Palm Beach Atlantic University and the University of Florida. (HSPBC.)

In order to carry bombs, the civilian planes had to be retrofitted with military bomb racks and bombsights. A technician at Morrison Field created one of the latter out of 20 cents' worth of scrap metal. Two holes were drilled into the flooring of the aircraft; one carried the wire to remove the safety, and the other wire released the bomb. The observer acted as the bombardier. The clearance between the bomb and the tarmac was only about seven inches, the length of a man's hand. Flying north along the sparsely populated coastline of Florida, the CAP aircraft has a 100-pound bomb mounted to its fuselage. The patrol routes for CP3 took the airplanes up to 60 miles off the coast, north to Cape Canaveral and south to Lantana, their starting point. (Both, HSPBC.)

Coastal Patrol 3's aircraft were constantly flying throughout the day. There was always a chance that a plane would malfunction while on patrol, and it happened that two of CP3's planes had to ditch in the ocean when their engines stopped working. One was 15 miles off of Jensen Beach, and the other was just off of Palm Beach; both crews found themselves members of the Duck Club—a CAP member who crashed landed into the water. It was no small job to keep track of the crews, their planes, the routes, and scheduled maintenance. The blackboard listed who was flying, which aircraft they were using, and the times of their flights, which lasted two hours each. Below, volunteer Imogen Parmelee plots an airplane's course. (Both, HSPBC.)

In May 1942, Coastal Patrol 3 moved seven miles south from Morrison Field to the new Lantana Airport. Expansion by the US Army's Air Transport Command necessitated the move. Lantana only had two runways, a small building used for administration offices, and a hangar's foundation. By the time this photograph was taken, two small buildings for communications and the canteen had been built, and tents for the mechanics were in place. Aircrews used the area west of the runways, currently the city of Atlantis, for bombing practice. An average of 76 men and women volunteered to man Coastal Patrol 3 at Lantana Airport, working together to protect the home front. (Both, HSPBC.)

The 112th Observation Squadron of the US Army Air Corps shared Lantana Airport with Coastal Patrol 3. The unit utilized O-47s and other aircraft to patrol Florida's coastal waters in conjunction with the CAP. The airplanes carried three crew members and had windows in the belly so the observers could see directly below their planes. The aircraft were also used to tow targets for gunnery practice. Coastal and antisubmarine patrols by the Army and CAP ended August 31, 1943, when the US Navy assumed the duty of patrolling the coast, and the threat from U-boats had diminished. The 112th transferred to Birmingham, Alabama, where it was deactivated, and the personnel were assigned to other units. (Both, HSPBC.)

Three

Boca Raton Army Air Field

In 1942, the Army Air Corps relocated its technical school for radar training to Boca Raton, Florida. Radar, an acronym for radio detection and ranging, was a new top secret technology at the time. A small airport stood just north of the present Glades Road to the west of downtown. Here, the land was relatively high and dry, yet close to the ocean and shipping lanes, and there was a good climate for flying.

The former Boca Raton Airport quickly grew, as hundreds of structures were constructed north of Palmetto Park Road to Yamato Road and from Dixie Highway to what is today the CSX (Amtrak) tracks. In addition, the military took over the exclusive Boca Raton Club for housing and classrooms from 1942 until 1944.

Boca Raton Army Air Field (BRAAF) offered classes for electronics and radar officers and related specializations for enlisted men. Thousands of men took their radar training at Boca Raton, including all the Army Air Forces' flight crews. Pop singer Tony Martin, some of the Tuskegee Airmen, and the crew of the *Enola Gay* all served a brief time at BRAAF.

Amongst the servicemen who trained at Boca Raton during the war were a significant number of African Americans, who were commonly housed and trained in separate facilities. Additionally, women enrolled in the Army Nurse Corps (ANC) and Women's Army Corps (WACs) served at BRAAF as nurses and in other technical capacities.

The impact of the presence of an important military facility on the little town of Boca Raton can hardly be imagined today. As many as 15,000 students came through each year between 1942 and 1944. In addition to the enlisted personnel, as many as 1,500 civilians were employed on the base at one time. The permanent population of Boca Raton was a little over 700 individuals. Every available room or house in town was rented.

In September 1947, a nasty hurricane demolished much of the base, and radar training relocated to Keesler Field, Biloxi, Mississippi. Today, the old runways are occupied by two important modern installations—Florida Atlantic University and the Boca Raton Airport.

The Army Air Forces Technical Training Command (AAFTC) established its new airborne radar training base in the small town of Boca Raton, Florida, in 1942. The unofficial mascot of the base was the flying pelican, shown diving through the air with radar waves emanating from his head. After war's end, the town's first newspaper was named the *Pelican* in its honor. (BRHSM.)

Initially, the AAFTC leased the exclusive Boca Raton Club as the headquarters for its new Boca Raton base. Constructed by famed architect Addison Mizner as the Cloister Inn in 1925, the club was greatly enlarged with additions by hotel architects Schultze and Weaver in 1929. In this photograph, air field officers inspect the beautiful grounds on the west side of the hotel in 1943. (BRHSM.)

In preparation for the military takeover, the Boca Raton Club staff scrambled to inventory and pack away the valuable furnishings and other features to protect them from damage by the soldiers. They also wrapped the gilt columns in the Cathedral Dining Room, one of the most beautiful spots in the hotel. (BRHSM.)

Lt. Col. Charles W. Skeele, Boca Raton Field commander, works at his desk at the Boca Raton Club in 1942. His office was located in a suite that was originally Mizner's Cloister Inn, located at the southeast corner of the hotel overlooking the Intracoastal Waterway. This is the portion of the hotel that was demolished around 1967 to make way for the famous 27-story tower. (BRHSM.)

The Boca Raton Club boasted two premier golf courses at the beginning of World War II. The north course was just west of the hotel and still stands. The south course was south of Camino Real and abandoned as a course during the war. Here, aviation cadets take time for a little rest and relaxation on the north course near the first tee, about 1942. (BRHSM.)

The Boca Raton Club's Schultze and Weaver–designed garden pool once welcomed socialites from northern climes. During the war, it served as a practice pool for water landings and sea rescues. In this photograph, the officers (well sheltered from Florida's sun) seem to be enjoying a fine day, while the cadets demonstrate their swimming prowess. (BRHSM.)

Air Cadet Alvin Thiele sent this postcard home to his parents in South Fallsburg, New York, in May 1943. In it, he gives a testimonial for the hotel that no publicity department could improve upon: "Pictures don't lie so here is what the club looks like. Only add a million beautiful colors and mild weather and there you have it. There are much larger grounds etc. around here too." Thiele also asked that his parents "keep this as a memory of my stay here in Boca Raton," which they did. Thiele himself presented the card to the Boca Raton Historical Society & Museum in 1986. (Both, BRHSM.)

A/C Alvin H. Thiele
Cadet B.T.C. #1
Squad. C Sect. 1903
Boca Raton Club, Room 210
Boca Raton, Fla.

BOCA RATON FIELD, FLA. MAY 9 7:30PM 1943

FREE

Dear Folks:

Pictures don't lie so here is just what the club looks like. Only add in a million beautiful colors and mild weather and there you have it. There are much larger grounds etc. around here too.

Keep this as a memory of my stay here in Boca Raton.

Love
Alvin

Mr. and Mrs. Thiele
Box 387
South Fallsburg,
New York

BRAAF military police (MPs) served local police departments in overseeing off-duty soldiers as far away as Fort Lauderdale during the war. Local towns were packed with servicemen, particularly at the bus stops and watering holes, and altercations and other offenses were bound to arise. Above, Jim McCrudden and Cal Messenger pose on Boca Raton's beach in 1945. At left, "Tex" Reed (left) and an unidentified MP take a break by their vehicle near the entrance to the Boca Raton Club in 1945. Although no longer leased by the government after 1944, the hotel still served as an active service center for BRAAF personnel. (Both, BRHSM.)

The town of Boca Raton, Florida, bore no resemblance then to the modern community it has become; the 1940 census reported 723 residents. There were practically no stores, only two bars and two sundry stores, a couple of gas stations, and no theaters or similar amenities. Life revolved around the glamorous Boca Raton Club and farmers growing green beans before the Boca Raton Army Air Field arrived in 1942. At right is a view looking north on Federal Highway from south of Palmetto Park Road, and below is a view looking south on Federal Highway from just north of Palmetto Park Road in the early 1940s. Please note there was indeed a traffic light. (Both, BRHSM.)

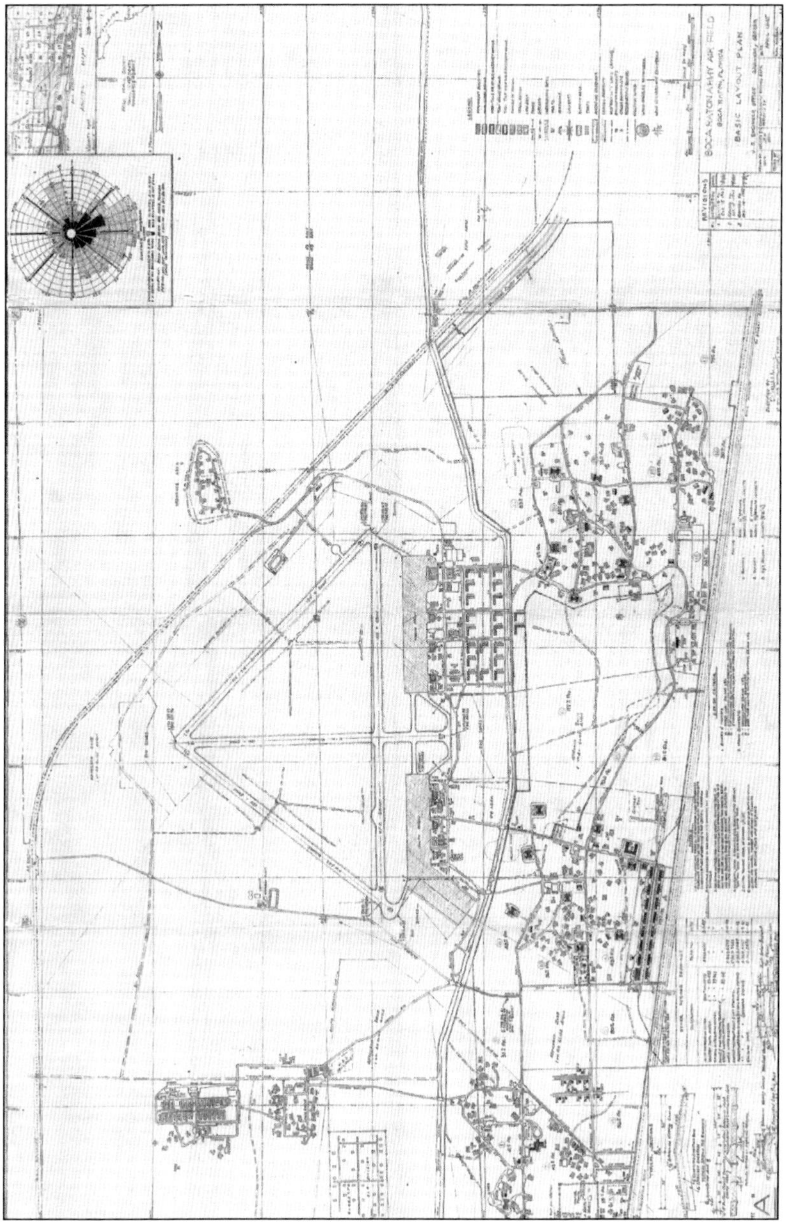

In May 1942, the government began acquisition of almost 6,000 acres of land for the Boca Raton Army Air Field. The site was chosen for its good flying weather, proximity to shipping lanes, and the existence of a small WPA-built airport located at the present site of Florida Atlantic University. The base extended from Palmetto Park Road on the south to north of Yamato Road and Dixie Highway on the east to what are today the CSX railroad tracks (near the present I-95) on the west. About 50 families and various property owners were displaced through the process known as eminent domain. The war department compensated all of the property owners—although few thought the amounts adequate. Over 800 buildings were constructed to serve every function—from school buildings and barracks to movie theaters and bowling alleys. Most were wooden and constructed hurriedly; others were made of a more readily available local material, concrete block. Today, only about 15 of the latter buildings survive. (BRHSM.)

The main entrance to the Boca Raton Army Air Field stood at Palmetto Park Road, just east of the intersection with NW Fourth Avenue on the north side of the road. This image shows the provost marshal's office at the official entrance. Note the flying pelican emblem, symbol of the field, atop the building's sign. (BRHSM.)

Col. Arnold MacSpadden was in charge of the design and construction of the cantonment at BRAAF. He employed what was known as the dispersed layout pattern for the buildings and streets of the base. Construction took place around existing trees and other features. The logic behind the irregular nature of the base layout was to minimize damage in case of strafing runs by enemy aircraft. (BRHSM.)

Lt. Gen. Barton Kyle Yount (in sunglasses) and other top brass of the Army Air Forces Technical Training Command (AAFTC) accompany base commander Col. Narcissus Lilli Cote (center) on an inspection tour of the Boca Raton Army Air Field January 1944. The building in the background, T602, served as a school building for the then top secret technology of radar. After the war, it became the Mizner Oaks Apartments, demolished in 2005. (BRHSM.)

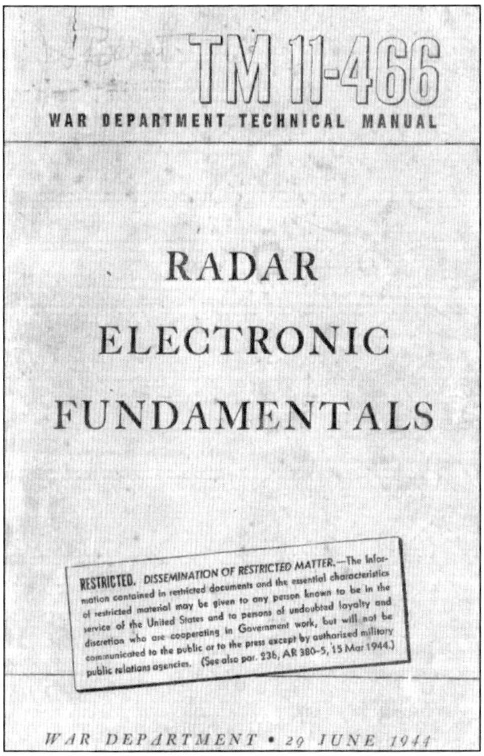

Radar, or radio detecting and ranging, was a top secret technology at the beginning of the war. According to the students who once trained at BRAAF, saying the word aloud could result in a court martial. They were not allowed to take notes in class, making learning the complicated technology rather challenging. Many students flunked out and went on to other assignments. This volume belonged to radar instructor James Barnt. (BRHSM.)

A group of radar instructors poses at the Boca Raton Army Air Field about 1944. Sgt. Bill Eddinger, shown at lower right, brought his wife and young daughter to Boca Raton from Pennsylvania in 1943. After the war, he and his family made their permanent home in the little town of Boca Raton. (BRHSM.)

A wide variety of airplanes provided training opportunities at the BRAAF installation. Charlie Bender became part of an aircrew after graduating from radar school, flying on B-25s and B-17s to check out the radio and radar equipment. Bender is pictured here in the copilot seat of a B-25 in 1945. (BRHSM.)

BRAAF's primary mission was to instruct airborne radar operators and mechanics, but there were also schools in high- and low-altitude bombing, radar navigation, airplane identification, attack interception, and survival training. These programs were expanded and adapted for peacetime in 1946–1947. In this image, students are seated at radar screens. (BRHSM.)

Two radar towers on the "ant line" appear to be the only survivors of this portion of BRAAF after the hurricane of September 1947. The antennae and nearby Quonset huts, which served as uncomfortable school buildings in the South Florida heat, were located on the south apron of the runway area. Today, this is the southeastern portion of the Florida Atlantic University campus. (BRHSM.)

Mechanics change a propeller on a Boeing B-17 Flying Fortress, one of the aerial workhorses of the war. It was first introduced in 1935, and more than 12,000 had been produced by war's end. The B-17 served in every combat zone during the conflict. Airplane mechanics ran complete inspections to ensure safety, and electronics mechanics were responsible for radio and radar communications systems at Boca Raton Field. (BRHSM.)

Unfortunately, a number of plane crashes caused the injury and even death of young crew members at Boca Raton Field before they had a chance to face the enemy. This image shows a wrecked B-34, notoriously difficult to fly, on the south end of the BRAAF runways in June 1943. (BRHSM.)

In this photograph, Lt. Manny Chavez briefs his crew before a radar-training mission. Chavez arrived in Boca Raton in early 1943, one of 25 newly minted pilots assigned to training in a variety of aircraft. The men practiced their radar skills by honing in on small boats and ships off Florida's east coast. (BRHSM.)

Crew members of a B-24 Liberator pose on the apron east of the runways at BRAAF around 1943. Like the B-17, the B-24 had four engines, and 10-member crews included a pilot, copilot, navigator, radioman, bombardier, ball turret gunners left and right, tail gunner, nose gunner, and flight engineer. (BRHSM.)

Former Civil Air Patrol pilot Orlo Maxfield was drafted into military service in 1944. Maxfield, a private and later a staff sergeant, was assigned to BRAAF in 1945 and became crew chief of his commanding officer's C-47 (a transport plane). He captured a close-up shot of one of the hangers at the base in this photograph from the mid-1940s. (BRHSM.)

Former aircraft assembly worker Pvt. (later Sgt.) Harry Magafan trained in radar and served as radar mechanic at BRAAF in 1943. Despite the warm earthbound weather of Boca Raton, Magafan is dressed for the cold clime above the clouds in an unheated aircraft in this photograph from June 1943. (BRHSM.)

Boca Raton Army Air Field provided many venues and environments for survival and combat training exercises, from sandy scrub to jungle marsh. Here, officers in the background observe a group of soldiers who are making their way under barbed-wire fences on the obstacle course amidst the scrub. Adding to the discomfort was a reasonable fear of diamondback rattlesnakes, fellow occupants of the area. (BRHSM.)

Survival training at BRAAF included an off-campus hike into the nearby Everglades. Paul Metro hiked for three days with a full backpack and an empty carbine. The soldiers slept in pup tents and took turns at guard duty. When a friend woke Metro during the night by touching his foot, Metro was frightened—as he thought it might be a snake. In this photograph, soldiers bivouac amidst some sabal palms. (BRHSM.)

Survival training for the men included unpleasant activities such as gas mask training to prepare for chemical warfare agents, including phosgene and mustard gas. Soldiers were subjected to regularly scheduled chemical assaults, which required the use of gas masks. Paul Metro recalled that on one occasion he "couldn't get his mask on quick enough and coughed for hours afterwards." These views show the soldiers entering a gas-filled chamber, above, and enduring a gas canister attack, below. The latter image was taken outside Mess Hall T651; today, this would be at the southwest corner of the intersection of Boca Raton Boulevard and NW Twentieth Street. (Both, BRHSM.)

The daily routine for the soldiers stationed at BRAAF began with PT (physical training), whatever the season or weather. For most of the year in Boca Raton, this meant high heat and high humidity—not necessarily something the men, coming from all over the United States, were at all accustomed to. Above, the men march in formation at PT Field 1, humorously nicknamed "Tojo's Graveyard," in sarcastic honor of Japan's wartime leader and the focus of much American hatred at the time. Below, the men take on the pull-up bars on the obstacle course, which was located north of today's Spanish River Boulevard at NW Fifth Avenue. (Both, BRHSM.)

Soldiers stationed at BRAAF underwent extensive firearms training, as at any other base. The view above shows a target box exercise in which men (lying on the ground in the foreground) take aim at paddles held over a target and secured on boxes at the opposite end of the room. The targets are immobilized by the men sitting astride the crates. In the view below, soldiers practice with M1 carbines, a lightweight alternative to the standard issue M1 rifle favored by soldiers with specialized training, such as flight crew members. They are on the rifle range located at the north end of the BRAAF. Today, this is the area just west of the Yamato Road interchange on I-95. (Both, BRHSM.)

There were at least 11 mess halls at BRAAF, serving food all day to thousands of hungry soldiers and visitors to the base. The line at Mess Hall 9 reveals not only AAF soldiers but a few sailors and even one civilian woman in the crowd. This mess hall was located on today's NW Fourth Avenue, where the playing field for Boca Christian School now stands. (BRHSM.)

Despite the long lines at the mess halls, not all soldiers found the offerings to their liking. Paul Metro recalled, "I thought the food was horrible." For breakfast, he ate only the boxed cereal, toast with butter or jam, and fruit—never the coffee or the scrambled eggs, which usually had, to Metro, a greenish tinge, which he attributed to the addition of saltpeter (potassium nitrate). (BRHSM.)

Cooking was serious business at a military base. Breads and cakes were baked in rack ovens like those shown here, where the cooks are checking out the latest batch of corn bread. A 1942 mess manual for corn bread calls for 9.5 pounds of corn meal, 2.25 pounds of flour, 3 ounces of baking powder, 3 ounces of salt, half a pound of fat, 20 eggs, 4 cans of evaporated milk, and 4 pints of water. (BRHSM.)

There were not too many options for a soldier if he got the munchies at BRAAF in the 1940s. Aside from the mess halls, with their long lines, only the service center featured any sort of restaurant or food service. There were no vending machines and only two sundry store/bars in the tiny town. In this photograph, Lew Hayes opts for raiding the refrigerator. (BRHSM.)

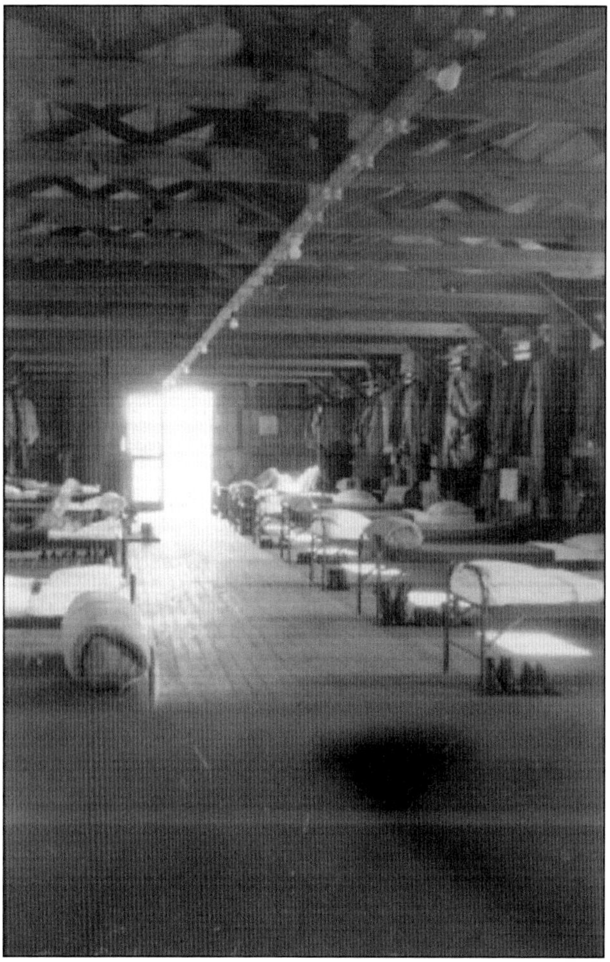

Most of the buildings at BRAAF, including the barracks, were made of simple wood-frame construction, covered with tar paper. In accordance with the dispersed layout plan, they were placed in seemingly random clusters through the eastern portions of the base. The landscaping consisted of sugar sand and whatever tree or bush happened to be there in the first place. The buildings were placed on block pilings for ventilation, access, and to keep out the local wildlife. Above, Phil Kantor (shirtless at left) poses with his bunkmates near their barracks in June 1945. At left is a rare view of the equally rustic interior of a barracks building, with the beds ready for inspection. (Both, BRHSM.)

In the days before air-conditioning, everyday life could be most uncomfortable in the South Florida heat and humidity. The summertime was particularly challenging; Ed Wallish recalled, "No matter how often you showered, it didn't take long to build up another sweat. It was impossible to change clothes more than once a day and everyone smelled from stale sweat." Although their uniforms were sent to the laundry, the men washed all their underwear and other personal items on wash day, as shown in the above photograph from 1944. Fortunately, the drying time was minimal in the hot Florida sun. Below, Harry Magafan scrubs his laundry the old-fashioned way in an image labeled "Typical GI life," from February 1944. (Both, BRHSM.)

BRAAF soldiers welcomed the presence of women on the base from its early days. These women of the Army Nurse Corps pose outside the station hospital in January 1943. Pictured here are, from left to right, Joy Barager, Anna Bell Longwater, Edna Schneider, Ruth Reid, Dorothy H. Hlucky, Louise Findley (chief nurse), Anne Maguire, Mary O'Connor, Rita McLarnan, Mervin McIntyre, Ruth Deese, Gladys Gillis, Ann Hooten, and Bernice Butler. (BRHSM.)

From left to right, Lts. Carolyn Ferguson, Glendora Pullen, Louise Findley, Dorothy Hlucky, Anne Maguire, and Mary O'Connor, Army Nurse Corps, pose with a Red Cross–provided vehicle outside the base hospital in November 1942. The hospital was located in the southwest corner of BRAAF, not far from the site of the present-day Meadows Park Pool. (BRHSM.)

Three unidentified nurses pose near the entrance to the nurses' quarters at BRAAF about 1943. Nurse Bernice Butler recalled she had a cot in an unair-conditioned, unheated barracks with an orange crate as a bedside table. The nurses arrived with no military training but were quickly taught military discipline and physical training to get them in shape. (BRHSM.)

Edith Mize Lewis poses outside the station hospital at BRAAF in 1942. Lewis, who was trained at BRAAF, eventually went on to become a flight nurse in the 816th Medical Evacuation Squadron of the 9th Air Force. Known as the "Flying Angel," she flew more than 50 missions near the front lines. Lewis prided herself that a soldier never died in her care. (BRHSM.)

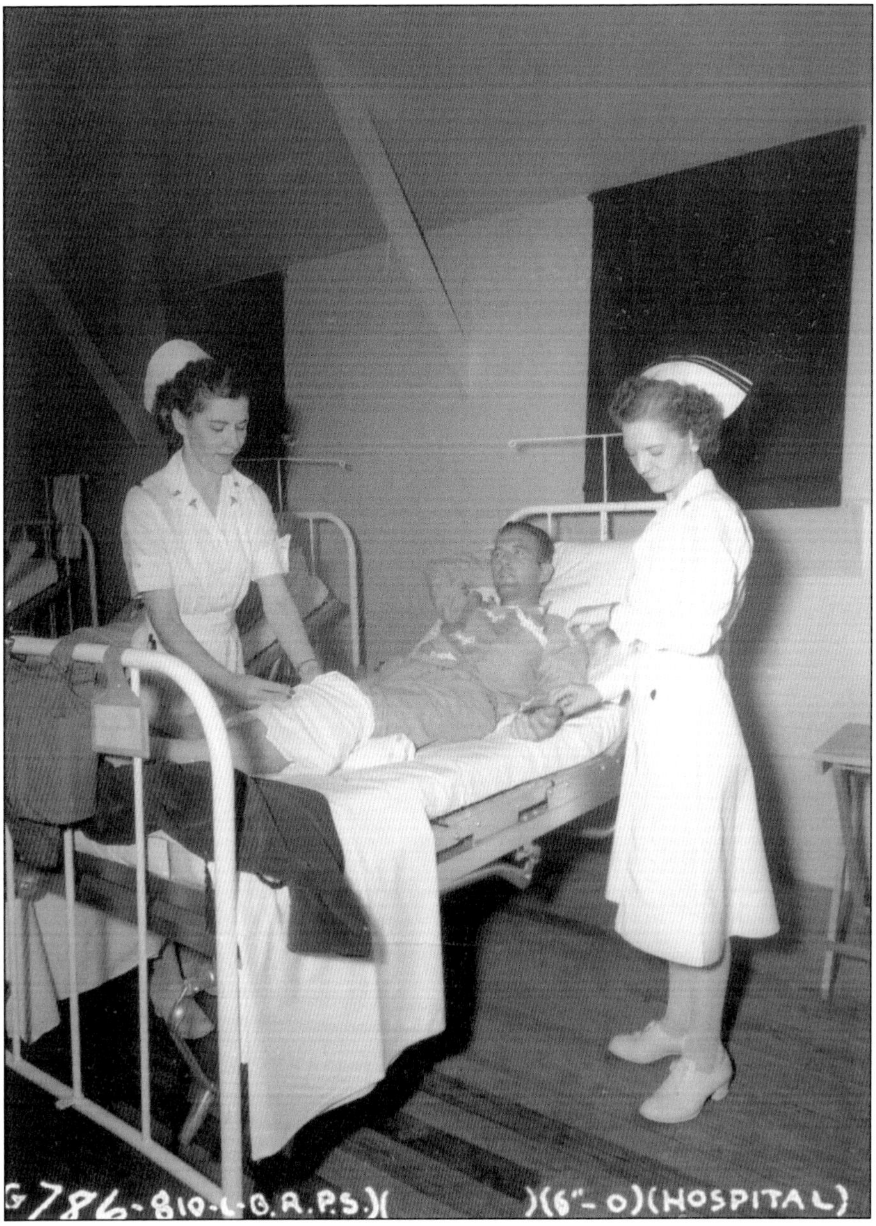

This official AAFTC photograph captures two nurses and a patient in this interior view of the 300-bed BRAAF hospital in 1943. When Lt. Bernice Butler arrived to work there in early 1943, she found the hospital terribly understaffed by doctors and nurses. She recalled that the doctors, although few in number, were "excellent, and had a good relationship with the patients." The nurses had to work 12-hour days, and conditions and medicines were primitive by modern standards. Sulfa drugs, not penicillin and antibiotics, were used to fight infections. Without breathing machines, nurses used paper sacks over the mouth and nose to stimulate deep breathing and prevent pneumonia in surgical patients. Although there were no battle wounds, nurses did deal with occasional plane crashes, car- and work-related injuries, rattlesnake bites, a variety of diseases and disorders, and much more pleasantly—babies born to military personnel and their families on the base. (USAFHRA.)

In May 1943, BRAAF received its first group of Women's Army Auxiliary Corps (WAACs), which became the Women's Army Corps (WACs) in July 1943. These women served in a wide variety of base support functions. WAC uniforms were notoriously ill-fitting and uncomfortable in the Florida climate, and women wore stockings and girdles at all times. These WACs do not seemed pleased to be suffering through yet another inspection. (BRHSM.)

WACs were housed separately from the men, on the southwest portion of BRAAF just east of the base hospital and nurses' quarters. Conditions were as spartan as they were for the men and nurses, but the women put their efforts into civilizing their living conditions by adding paint and curtains. In this view of the WAC mess, note the presence of tablecloths—in contrast to the general men's mess. (BRHSM.)

An unidentified WAC poses with Maj. Dean Lindstrom and an unidentified airman at BRAAF, around 1943. Lindstrom was the special service officer, in charge of entertainment for the field. Special services support was a typical WAC assignment. A large field like BRAAF boasted a regular round of activities, including performances, dances, and speeches to keep the soldiers happy and out of trouble. (BRHSM.)

A WAC repairs a radio at BRAAF in June 1943. Additionally, WACs at BRAAF worked as clerks and in other capacities in payroll, statistics, the post office, the PX, and the orderly room and as supply and switchboard clerks, cooks, cryptographers, librarians, photographers, teletype and radio operators, hospital ward workers, dental assistants, medical lab technicians, plane dispatchers, drivers, and mechanical and repair workers. (USAFHRA.)

Squadron F members gather for a photograph about 1947. During World War II, segregation was still very much a part of life, including in the military. At BRAAF, African American soldiers were assigned to Squadron F and housed in separate facilities on the northeastern portion of the base. They also had their own PX and entertainment facilities. Pres. Harry S. Truman ordered the desegregation of the military in 1948. (BRHSM.)

African American soldiers observe instruction on the parts of a machine gun at BRAAF around 1943. There were no black officers assigned at BRAAF; instructors were white. Archie Carswell recalled, "We were all on the base there together, but we could not eat at the same place and we could not have recreation or training together . . . I felt that we were both fighting the war so we should fight together." (BRHSM.)

BRAAF had three chapels to cater to the spiritual needs of those stationed there. They were, like others on the base, wooden buildings, but constructed with high arched beams and designed for beauty, not just function. In addition to Sunday services, the chapels hosted a number of weddings and even baptisms for military personnel. (USAFHRA.)

Many a romance began at the Boca Raton Army Air Field during World War II. One of the longest lasting was that of Lt. Bernice Butler, Army Nurse Corps, and Lt. (later Lt. Col.) Manny Chavez. They met and were married in a chapel on the base in July 1943. Their marriage lasted 71 years. (BRHSM.)

Irene Demery was born in the little town of Boca Raton, Florida, the daughter of one of the town's earliest African American pioneer families. She got a wartime job at the Squadron F post exchange; it was there she met the love of her life, Pvt. Archie Carswell. Irene is pictured here in front of a patriotic-themed backdrop at a Delray Beach photography studio sometime between 1942 and 1945. (BRHSM.)

Pvt. Archie Carswell, originally of Cairo, Georgia, was stationed at BRAAF from 1942 to 1943. His job was to transport new equipment on and off base and drive cadets to and from the train depot and Boca Raton Club. Archie met and married Irene Demery in 1943, and they returned to live in Boca Raton after the war. The couple, married for 68 years, were separated only by death. (BRHSM.)

Col. Frank Fisher Jr. of LaGrange, Illinois, and later Vero Beach, Florida, had reached the rank of captain during World War I. After that conflict, he was an executive for Marshall Field & Company. That experience served him well when he patriotically campaigned to reenter military service in 1942. After corresponding with the FBI and various US senators, Fisher was appointed a major and landed the position of post exchange officer for BRAAF in 1942, where he ultimately rose to the rank of lieutenant colonel. Fisher was apparently well liked by his staff as evidenced by his wartime scrapbook, full of lighthearted cartoons about him. Above, Fisher works at his desk on the base around 1943. Below, Fisher is depicted showing his poor opinion of soldier intoxication by one of his staff members. (Both, BRHSM.)

BRAAF continued to operate as an important radar training facility after the war's end. There was allegedly some discussion of making Boca Raton a permanent Air Force installation; however, all such thoughts came to an end when a Category 4 hurricane swept ashore near Fort Lauderdale on September 17, 1947. The large, slow-moving storm also brought widespread flooding to the area. This was followed by another hurricane on October 12. The resulting flood covered all of southeast Florida. The widespread destruction was an amazing sight to behold; everyone in Boca Raton with a camera came out to document the storm, judging from the hundreds of photographs that survive today. Above is one of the damaged hangars by the runway; below, a popular view shows barracks felled by the high storm winds. (Both, BRHSM.)

THE TRANSMITTER

By and For the Personnel of Boca Raton Army Air Field

Thursday, 2 October, 1947 — BOCA RATON, FLORIDA — Volume V—No. 32

MOVE TO KEESLER FIELD BEGINS

Fire Prevention Week, October 5-11

FIRE PREVENTION WEEK TO BE OBSERVED HERE

President Truman, several state governors and the governor-general of Canada have proclaimed the week of Oct. 5-11, 1947, as Fire Prevention Week. The increase in loss of life and property by fire since World War II has made this current campaign more important than any in history.

Percy Bugbee, general manager of the National Fire Prevention Association said today that "in the face of the country's worst housing shortage, we are burning up enough timber and lumber annually to build two hundred thousand five room houses." A study by the FPA reveals that the average American family of five will pay a 1947 fire tax of over $50 on the basis of the $700,000,000 fire loss forecast by this group plus indirect fire costs that double the total.

Last year approximately 11,000 persons burned to death while a total of more than 20,000 persons were injured in fires. Fire authorities charge that needless fires are seriously jeopardizing the national economy and reported that there were over 600,000 building ...

Quick Acting Driver Saves Life-Property

(Editor's Note: The story of the fire in Bldg. 2006 in last week's edition of the Transmitter, was based entirely on the facts gathered from Fire Station number one and covered only one angle of the story. It was later learned that there were more important angles not brought to light. In the following account taken from an interview with Sgt. Clark at the Base Motor Pool, a member of ...

Dear Colonel White:

I wish to take this opportunity on behalf of the Town of Boca Raton, and the people from the surrounding communities who took shelter during the storm in the Boca Raton Club, to thank you for the food and other services which were rendered.

I can assure you that the preparations made by the Field for the convenience of the people were greatly appreciated, and many have expressed their gratitude.

Yours very truly,
J. C. MITCHELL,
Mayor,
Town of Boca Raton

SCHOOL, 669TH BAND TO BE MOVED BY 15 DEC.

As per a directive from Air Training Command Headquarters at Barksdale Field, Louisiana, the move to Keesler was started this week. In light of the Hurricane damage on the field, it is General Cannon's desire to have the base moved as quickly as possible.

If plans for the move work out as scheduled the 3501st Base Unit and the 669th Army Air Force Band will be cleared from the field by December 15th. The Band will be moved intact while the 3501st Base Unit will be separated, the permanent party men not connected directly with the Radar School being segregated into other fields of the Training Command.

Men of Squadron K-2, caught by our roving photog airing their "unmentionables" after being "washed out" by the recent BIG BLOW.

New Assistant At Service Club

Tech Library Is Open For All

The October 2, 1947, issue of the base newspaper, the *Transmitter*, documents the removal of BRAAF to its new location at Keesler Field in Biloxi, Mississippi. Damage to the base from the September hurricane, estimated at $3 million, hurried this process. Capt. James Vaughter was one of those assigned to help close the base. Knowing that the balance in the officers' club funds were to be sent to Washington for the general fund, the remaining officers decided to have a big bash at the Boca Raton Club, former home of BRAAF. As Vaughter later recalled, "Flaming food was served, and we had a waiter for each couple. Danny Kaye was at the hotel that night." What became the US Air Force continued to maintain a small auxiliary installation at the runways of the base until 1959, with a few officers and its own fire department, which staffed fire rescue units. (BRHSM.)

The loss of BRAAF and its personnel was a terrific blow to Boca Raton's economy. However, it had an unimagined positive side as well. The War Assets Administration sold much of the former base acreage and its surviving buildings to a variety of developers and entrepreneurs in the 1950s. This sparked a postwar commercial boom, aided by the return of thousands of former servicemen to the area seeking a permanent home in sunny South Florida. Above, Domina Jalbert, an aerologist responsible for the parafoil design, made his headquarters in a former T-building on NW Twentieth Street. Below, a similar building on Spanish River Boulevard was converted into the Southland Apartments. A number of these former radar school structures survive in Boca Raton today. (Both, BRHSM.)

Looking north from the area of Glades Road, these two aerial views show the runways on the northwest section of the Boca Raton Army Airfield during World War II and in 2012. The west-pointing triangle of the runway is barely visible today. Boca Raton was able to acquire this property from the government after the war and use it to lure the newest state university to town—Florida Atlantic University. FAU opened its doors in October 1964, making an ongoing impact on the community far beyond that of its predecessor, BRAAF. In the upper left corner of the triangle is the Boca Raton Airport, another legacy of BRAAF. (Above, BRHSM; below, Peter Lorber and Courtenay Gilbert.)

Four

Hooligans and More

There were several other military facilities in Palm Beach County besides Morrison Field and BRAAF, although none were as large or hosted as many soldiers. Members of Coast Guard Temporary Reserve Flotilla 3, Division 2, were proud to call themselves members of the "Hooligan Navy," a derogatory term used by regular US Navy and Coast Guard personnel. The men, who were not otherwise fit for military service, donated their time for training and patrols, while maintaining their regular jobs. With the reserve's less restrictive age and physical requirements, this was the one service they could provide, and it released regular Coast Guardsmen for overseas combat duty. They used the Coast Guard facility on Peanut Island and another location at the north end of West Palm Beach as their base of operation.

Their sister organization, the SPARs, was housed in Palm Beach at the Biltmore Hotel, which was used by the US Navy as a hospital during the last months of the war. The SPARs used to march in formation, carrying their towels to the beach for physical training up Sunrise Avenue, and conducted parade drills on the Breakers' golf course. Also in Palm Beach, the US Army leased the Breakers and converted it into Ream General Army Hospital.

Camp Higgins, a US Army encampment, was housed at the north end of the island on the inlet. The local newspapers reported that soldiers from that facility participated in baseball and basketball games against soldiers from other military facilities. They also took part in parades on Worth Avenue and Clematis Street. There were reportedly 150-millimeter gun emplacements at Camp Higgins, along with some tanks. Unfortunately, no images have yet been found.

Farther west, near Belle Glade, a prisoner-of-war camp existed for nine months. The prisoners had been sent from Camp Blanding in northern Florida to help with the bean harvest and canning. A national brouhaha ensued when the prisoners went on strike after a snafu had held up provisions for the PX and no one, neither prisoners nor guards, could purchase cigarettes. Sadly, no images of the camp have been found.

Gleason Stambaugh (1905–1979), owner of Florida Music Company, donated his time and boat to Coast Guard Auxiliary Flotilla 3, Division 2. By the end of the war, he commanded 1,700 regular and temporary reserve Coast Guardsmen in Palm Beach County. In 1942, he encountered what he identified as an Italian submarine, which immediately dove underwater. Stambaugh was grateful for this timid retreat, as his boat only carried a shotgun—no match for the deck cannons on the sub. The men used their own boats (some carried depth charges and .50-caliber machine guns) to patrol offshore during the night, watching for stricken vessels and German submarines. They were also responsible for security at the Port of Palm Beach, maintaining coastal watch towers, patrolling the beach by horseback and on foot, and manning the bridges crossing Lake Worth, checking everyone's identification. (Both, HSPBC.)

The Coast Guardsmen retrieved merchant sailors after their ships had been destroyed by U-boats as well as the bodies of those who did not survive the attacks. Local residents and the American Red Cross would feed, clothe, and house the survivors until they could arrange transportation to their home ports. The Coast Guard also worked to recover any useful flotsam from the stricken ships. (HSPBC.)

The Barrett family owned a group of tourist cottages south of Palmetto Park Road in Boca Raton known as the Boca Raton Villas. Today, this is the site of the Beresford Condominium. So much flotsam came ashore from the torpedoed merchant ships in 1942 that the Barretts were able to sell salvaged rubber to the government. Here, Peter and Martha Barrett pose for a photograph during the war, with young Peter sporting uniform-inspired attire. (BRHSM.)

Founded on November 23, 1942, the US Coast Guard Women's Reserve was created so men could be released from stateside duties for combat. At first, the women were called WARCOGS, but they were soon renamed SPARs after the Coast Guard's motto: *Semper Paratus* (Always Ready). By 1946, there were 10,000 women who had joined the SPARs. Many served as clerks, but others worked as parachute riggers, cooks, pharmacist's mates, vehicle drivers, and radiomen. At the converted 430-room Biltmore Hotel, 900 women started SPAR enlisted training in June 1943. It was the largest enlisted SPAR training station, and although it was open only 18 months, more than 7,000 women graduated from the six-week basic training course. In the photograph below, the SPARs band poses outside of St. Edward's Catholic Church. The US Navy converted the Biltmore into a naval hospital. (Both, HSPBC.)

Expecting a large number of wounded from the invasion of Africa, the US Army leased the Breakers Hotel for $250,000 per year and converted it into a hospital, which opened in December 1942. With its wide hallways and large elevators, the hotel was easily transformed into a 500-bed hospital that specialized in neuropsychiatry and plastic surgery. Rich carpets and brocade hangings were removed, and some chandeliers were replaced with GI lights. The south loggia of the hotel became an officers' lounge, the ballroom became the recreation hall, the mezzanine was turned into operating rooms, and the Cocoanut Grove room became a dental clinic. About 750 patients and 400 military personnel resided at the hotel. It also served servicemen's family members, and several babies were born at Ream General Hospital. Returned to the owners, the resort reopened on December 11, 1944. (Both, HSPBC.)

After being cooped up at Ream General Hospital recovering from war wounds, servicemen are offered an escape by the Red Cross Motor Corp and the hospital motor pool. The men were packed into trucks and driven south of the hospital down South Ocean Boulevard to the Palm Beach Pier and the beach. The soldiers spent their newfound freedom sunbathing on the beach and swimming in the warm waters of the Atlantic Ocean. Others relaxed on the pier and enjoyed the sun while still others tried their luck at fishing. If the beach did not excite some of the men, then they could always stroll down Palm Beach's famous Worth Avenue, which was right across the street from the pier. (Both, HSPBC.)

Located on the Jupiter Inlet Lighthouse grounds, US Navy Station J monitored the low-frequency radio transmissions of U-boats. The messages were then sent to Washington for code breaking and translation. Several such listening stations would vector in where the submarines were located, directing naval aircraft, which then destroyed the enemy U-boats. In May and June 1943, sixty-seven submarines were destroyed in nearby Atlantic waters. (FSA.)

Special Army "A" Award Edition

THE EVERGLADES NEWS

$22,000,000 FROM 84,000 ACRES

1942-43 CROP SEASON

The VAST AGRICULTURAL EMPIRE ON THE SHORE OF LAKE OKEECHOBEE IS RESPONSIBLE FOR PALM BEACH COUNTY WINNING THE ARMY "A" AWARD FOR PRODUCTION

The Army "A" Award For Agricultural Achievement Will Be Awarded Palm Beach County Farmers In A Special Ceremony Monday, November 29, 1943 At 10 A. M.

More than 9,000 German prisoners were held in Florida. From March to December 1945, about 250 POWs were interned at a camp just east of Belle Glade, where they worked in a bean-canning factory. Two weeks after arriving, the prisoners initiated a strike when their cigarette rations were reduced, outraging the public nationwide. Strikers were restricted to bread and water until they returned to work. (HSPBC.)

On July 5, 1942, officials dedicated Camp Murphy, the US Army's Southern Signal Corps School. The site was named for Signal Corps officer Lt. Col. William H. Murphy, who was killed in action in the Far East in February 1942. From its conception in January 1942, the school took only six months to construct. The base was located along Highway US 1 in southern Martin County, just north of Jupiter. (FSA.)

Soldiers from Camp Murphy formed their own theatrical group and called themselves the Camp Murphy Players. They performed at various venues, including the Paramount Theater in Palm Beach, where they supported the war bond drive with a performance of *The Army Day by Day*. Given to the state after the war, the property is now Jonathan Dickinson State Park. (HSPBC.)

Five

Civilians at Work

In 1942, the citizens of Palm Beach County found the enemy at their doorstep when they experienced a series of German submarine attacks on merchant shipping just off the coast. U-boats sank 24 ships off the coast of Florida, 16 of them between Cape Canaveral and Boca Raton from February through May 1942. Citizens covered their windows with blackout curtains and darkened their headlights in the night hours to avoid providing a target for the enemy offshore.

Along the beaches and atop tall buildings, each community posted aircraft watch stations manned by local civilians and military wives. Members of the Aircraft Warning Service included young and old, men and women. They memorized the silhouettes of both Axis and Allied aircraft and manned their stations during daylight hours to document any aircraft flying overhead. The Boca Raton tower, located on a then-deserted beachfront, was outfitted with a telephone line in case the volunteers spotted a plane or submarine.

The influx of military installations proved a great boon to local economies during the war. Every hostelry and even ordinary homeowners patriotically and profitably opened their doors to the military spouses, families, and even civilian workers desperate for a domicile from 1942 to 1947. Two housing projects were constructed in Boca Raton by the Federal Housing Authority in 1943, just to try and keep up with the influx of residents.

Civilians volunteered in different capacities to support the war effort, and some decided to loan their homes. In 1942, Amy (Phipps) Guest offered her palatial Palm Beach house, Villa Artemis, to the Navy for use as a convalescent hospital for officers. In November 1942, Navy Lt. Cmdr. Melvin Stover took charge of the house.

In every goal set by the National American Red Cross for individual chapters, from people trained in first aid to fundraising, Palm Beach County exceeded its quota. The Red Cross assisted military families in need with loans, medical assistance, and housing. It was a vital civilian-based service that was eagerly supported by patriotic civilians, military spouses, and the soldiers themselves.

Helen Maass (third from left, top) volunteered with the American Red Cross as chairman of the nutrition committee, which helped housewives serve nutritious meals using local fruits and vegetables and what they could purchase with their ration coupons. She also helped prepare bandages and worked in the Volunteers for Victory Canteen for enlisted men on the corner of Worth Avenue and County Road. The Morrison Field Woman's Club served as the Red Cross headquarters at the base. Many of the women volunteers had spouses stationed at the field, and they learned how to repair the vehicles they used. With gas rationing leaving many families without transportation, the motor corps drove volunteers to their posts, transported civilians to medical appointments, and took convalescing servicemen and women on outings. (Both, HSPBC.)

BRAAF officers' wives, civilians, and soldiers themselves participated in activities to benefit the American Red Cross during World War II. In this humorous photograph, Mrs. John Walker suffers the tender ministrations of, from left to right, Mrs. Richard H. Becker, Mrs. Richard Dawkins, Mrs. Joe M. Cook, and Mrs. Frank F. Fisher Jr., in 1943. (BRHSM.)

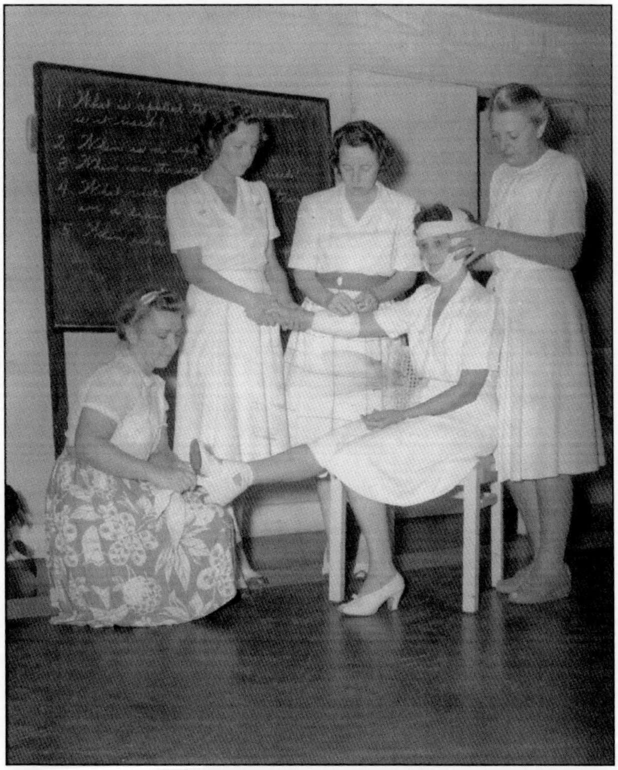

The Red Cross served as an emergency relief agency for American families during the war, providing moral as well as financial support to the wives of servicemen. BRAAF featured at least four Red Cross buildings during the conflict. Here, an unidentified soldier joins Ira Patton and Reece Jones, staff members of the local ARC, outside the BRAAF ARC headquarters near the Florida East Coast Railway tracks between 1942 and 1943. (BRHSM.)

Individuals and businesses helped the war effort by collecting scrap metal, rubber, paper, and other items used to manufacture war supplies such as small arms, tanks, and planes. In 1942, the Scrap Producer Merit Award was awarded to Gagon Auto Parts. Pictured here presenting the award to owner A.F. Gagon (wearing hat) are, from left to right, Marvin Mounts, West Palm Beach mayor J.O. Bowen, and auto salvage inspector C.M. King. Students and schools also participated in scrap competitions. During a statewide competition in 1942, Palm Beach High School student Gwendolyn Willcocks, 15, collected 101,116 pounds of scrap metal. She and the other winners were part of a delegation sent to Mobile, Alabama, for the dedication and launching of the Liberty ship *Colin P. Kelly Jr.*, named for a Florida airman killed in action in 1941. (Above, HSPBC; left, FSA.)

The need for metals for the war effort launched a nationwide scrapping campaign. Schools, organizations, and individuals competed to see who could collect the most scrap in a month. The State of Florida challenged schools to collect as much scrap metal as they could. After a month of scavenging, schools in Loxahatchee and Greenacres, in Palm Beach County, and Cape Florida, in Dade County, emerged as the top Florida schools. Each sent representatives to Mobile, Alabama, for the launching of the Liberty ship *Colin P. Kelly Jr.* The representatives and individual winners met with former governor Fred Cone before traveling to Mobile. Pictured here are, from left to right, Albert Thompson (Loxahatchee), Betty Lou Smith (Coral Gables), Governor Cone, Dale Maxwell (Pahokee), Gwendolyn Willcocks (Palm Beach High), Joseph Thibodeaux (Greenacres), and Allen Shelton (Cape Florida). At the 1942 launching ceremony in Mobile, Dale Maxwell of Pahokee, who personally collected a staggering 202,650 pounds of scrap metal, says a few words. (Both, FSA.)

Civilians formed a significant part of the workforce at the Boca Raton Army Air Field. As many as 1,500 were employed at one time, and it was an excellent opportunity for local women's employment. Workers came from as far as West Palm Beach and Fort Lauderdale, assisting in the academic, quartermaster, and engineering departments. Richard and Eldra Durham of Fort Lauderdale both served as postal clerks at the base from 1943 to 1947, working 10- and 11-hour days. At left, Fort Lauderdale resident Eldra Durham runs mail through the meter. Below, an unidentified civilian woman instructs soldiers about radios in 1943. (Left, BRHSM; below, USAFHRA.)

During the war, civilians of the Aircraft Warning Service (AWS) manned aircraft-spotting towers in coastal areas along the Atlantic, Gulf of Mexico, and Pacific. Boca Raton's spotting tower was located on the beach just north of the present Red Reef golf course. The spotters memorized the silhouettes of both Allied and Axis aircraft and kept lookout for aircraft and submarines. This was a patriotic duty that both young and old could perform; youngsters often accompanied their mothers in the after-school shift. At right, two women pose atop Boca Raton's tower, which was demolished in 1946. Below is a typical aircraft spotter's guide from October 1942. (Both, BRHSM.)

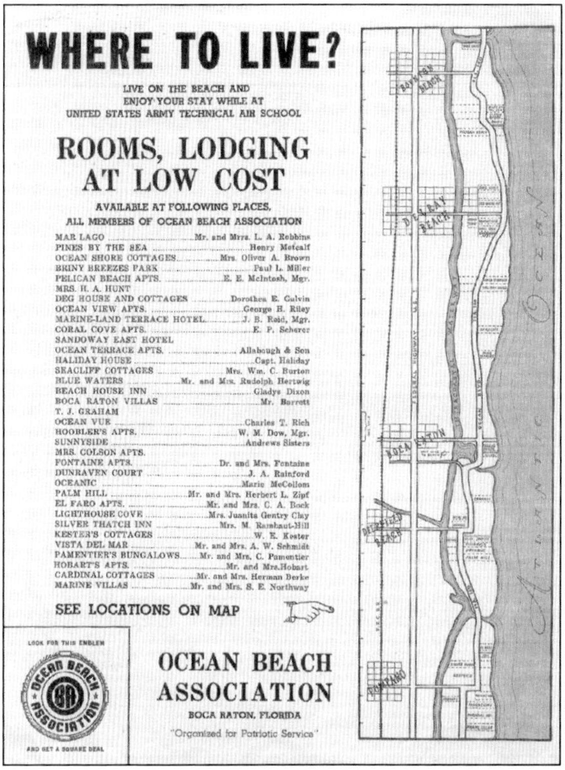

Many of the soldiers stationed at the Boca Raton Army Air Field, particularly the officers and instructors, came with their families in tow. There was minimal housing to be had in town, and lodging was at a premium during wartime. This map indicates local hostelries and boardinghouses available along the beachfront from as far north as Boynton Beach to as far south as Pompano Beach in 1942. (BRHSM.)

During the war, Lillian Williams ran a popular boarding establishment in a small wooden cottage known as Singing Pines in Boca Raton. She erected cardboard partitions to create more rooms and slept on the porch to accommodate more lodgers. She even housed two families, each with babies, in her garage. Here, Lillian's mother, Nellie Race (seated), also an occupant of Singing Pines, poses with other lodgers in 1942. (BRHSM.)

Off-base housing for Boca Raton Army Air Field personnel ranged from derelict to divine. So crunched was the community that two federal housing projects were constructed in 1943. The Palmetto Park Project, pictured above in the 1950s, was located on the south side of Palmetto Park Road and west of the Florida East Coast Railway tracks and served the white community. Dixie Manor, on Dixie Highway north of Glades Road, was built for the African American community, and it still stands. The command staff at BRAAF was able to afford slightly finer accommodations. Colonel Fisher and his family rented the house shown below in the exclusive Estates section of Boca Raton. Originally designed by Palm Beach architect Maurice Fatio in the 1930s, it is now in the National Register of Historic Places. (Both, BRHSM.)

Alexander Scavnicky worked as the caretaker for Harold Vanderbilt's oceanfront house, Eastover, in Manalapan, Florida. Scavnicky, his wife, Anna, and their daughter Alexandra lived on the property and had front-row seats to the U-boat activities offshore. Vanderbilt's 1930 Maurice Fatio–designed house was one of the first built in Manalapan, which was incorporated in 1931 by Vanderbilt and named after Manalapan Township, New Jersey. A few years later, Vanderbilt's sister, Consuelo Vanderbilt Balsan, the former Duchess of Marlborough, built a house just to the west on Hypoluxo Island. Winston Churchill visited Balsan there after the war and spent his time resting and painting. (Both, HSPBC)

Six

THAT'S ENTERTAINMENT!

Keeping thousands of military men and women occupied during their off hours was an important priority for the local installations and surrounding communities during World War II. Both the Special Services Office and civilian organizations put together a continuous round of dances, performances, parties, tournaments, and sporting activities. In addition to keeping the troops occupied, these events proved to be an important bonding opportunity with the permanent local residents.

The Boca Raton Army Air Field band provided much of the musical entertainment in and around Boca Raton during the war. Originally formed by a core of professional Miami musicians, it grew to 170 members and performed as a marching band, an orchestra, and a dance band at functions on and off base. These musicians were culled from the most famous of the big bands of the era and brought a never-before-seen level of professional entertainment to the local populace. Pop singer and Special Services officer Tony Martin served at BRAAF, hosting weekly variety shows. A number of famous African American performers such as Cab Calloway's pianist, Benny Payne, also shared their talents for the packed crowds. Music seems to have been the one arena in which the white and black communities came together in those days of segregation. Black performers would play at the white venues, and the BRAAF band often entertained at the "Colored USO" in Delray Beach.

Competitive sports found active participants as well as spectators amongst servicemen in the area. Individual squadrons often formed their own baseball, basketball, bowling, and football teams and played each other as well as with other military bases. The BRAAF football team even went up against the University of Miami Hurricanes twice in 1943. Amateur boxing was a very popular sport at the Boca Field; bouts were held on Monday nights and divided into weight classes.

The heart of BRAAF's entertainment was the enlisted men's service club. It featured a dance floor, well-stocked music room, library, cafeteria, and soda fountain. Soldiers could play horseshoes, ping-pong, archery, chess, card games, or simply enjoy reading and writing.

Servicemen and women found themselves in the Palm Beaches for a variety of reasons. The one thing they all wanted was entertainment. A popular venue was the Volunteers for Victory Soldier Canteen at H. Butterfield Company grocery store at South County Road and Worth Avenue in Palm Beach. Here, a military band performs outside the canteen for military and civilian spectators in preparation for a parade down Worth Avenue. (HSPBC.)

At the V for Victory Canteen, soldiers could relax and socialize with the pretty waitresses or get directions to the beach just a block away. They could grab quick a meal and something to drink or relax in the canteen's reading room. In a six-month period, the canteen served over 42,000 sandwiches to hungry GIs. (HSPBC.)

In 1941, Ted Stone opened Ta-bóo, at 221 Worth Avenue in Palm Beach. Legend has it that it got its name from Stone, who liked to say "That's taboo" when anyone said anything disagreeable. Military officers from Morrison Field frequented Ta-bóo and were treated to good times by some of the regulars at the restaurant. The restaurant continues to be a hangout for royalty, actors, astronauts, and politicians. (HSPBC.)

The town of Boca Raton, population a little more than 700 people at the time, boasted two bars during World War II. One was Brown's (also a restaurant and sundry store), located on Federal Highway just south of Palmetto Park Road, at the site of the present-day Flanigan's. In this photograph, soldiers enter the establishment while some hitch a ride out of town—north to civilization—sometime during the war years. (BRHSM.)

The Third AAF Band (later the 503rd AAF Band) at the Boca Raton Army Air Field was founded in 1942. Band leader Maurice Shorago, a service pilot, flew around the country recruiting celebrity musicians for BRAAF. The band eventually grew to 170 members and provided outstanding professional-quality entertainment the likes of which the residents of the little farming town of Boca Raton had never seen. (BRHSM.)

A group of professional Miami musicians provided the core of the BRAAF band in 1942, exchanging their jazz music for military marches. The sax octet shown here is composed of those original Miami musicians (with the exception of nonnative Proctor): from left to right, Harry C. Amidon, Charles J. Proctor Jr., Oley W. Dietz, Harris T. Freeman, Sidney T. Freeman, James Williams, Theodore F. Lee, and Stanley Biedron. (BRHSM.)

BRAAF band members join Lt. Ken Jones at the piano in 1943. Pictured here are, from left to right, SSgt. "Flea" Madden, Sergeant Croughan, Sgt. Lou Tollison, SSgt. Bernie Gluckman, Staff Sergeant Freeman, Sgt. "Pinkie" Feasel, Sergeant Knott, Sgt. Jack Laubach, TSgt. Bill Clark, SSgt. John Huebner, Sgt. Bob Thew, Sgt. Wes Asbury, Private Koenig, Sgt. Charles Proctor, Sgt. Jack Lacey, Sgt. Miff Frink, and SSgt. Theodore Lee. (BRHSM.)

Zack Mosley, famous cartoonist and creator of the long-running comic *The Adventures of Smilin' Jack*, penned this drawing of a wartime beauty as a tribute to the BRAAF band in 1943. The inscription reads, "Sweet stuff landings to the Boca Raton 'in the groovers' from Cindy and Zack Mosely." (BRHSM.)

Floridian Bill Cooke (1905–2003), right, traveled the country playing in washboard bands, with most winters spent in West Palm Beach. Locally, he performed with the West Palm Beach Washboard Band, playing in the streets, theaters, and private Palm Beach homes. The band was on *The Today Show* in the 1960s. Moving to West Palm Beach permanently in 1973, Cooke continued to entertain until his death. (HSPBC.)

Entertainment venues opened throughout Palm Beach County to provide places for servicemen and women to unwind. Most places offered food, drink, a reading library, and music. These recreational places also offered a chance to mingle with others. Here, soldiers, sailors, WAACs, and SPARs gather around a piano for a sing-along. (HSPBC.)

One of the most important structures on all of BRAAF was the service club for enlisted men. A large, two-story structure, it was located on the NW Fourth Diagonal in Boca Raton. The first event there was a Christmas dance held on December 23, 1942. It featured a large tree on the balcony above the fireplace (right). The event was clearly well attended (below), and the BRAAF band provided music for the occasion. In addition to dances, movies, and performances, the clubhouse offered ping-pong, billiards, cards, horseshoes, arts and crafts, and a variety of diversions for the soldiers. After the war, this became Moody Hall, a dormitory for the Bibletown Christian resort. (Both, USAFHRA.)

From 1942 until 1944, the Boca Raton Club served as the officers' club for the officers of BRAAF. Once the lease on the hotel ended, a new facility was constructed on the base at the site of today's Boca Christian School on NW Fourth Avenue. The opening on July 4, 1945, was a grand occasion. The command staff "meeted and greeted" base officers and their wives at a reception, followed by dinner and dancing with music provided by the BRAAF band. Above, an exterior view of the officer's club shows alfresco diners on the covered patio. Below, officers and wives get a chance to socialize in the very 1940s-style interior. Note the fireplace at left, a somewhat unusual feature for a Florida building of the time. (Both, BRHSM.)

Sporting activities proved an important diversion for soldiers at the field as well as the townies in Boca Raton. BRAAF formed several football teams, which played each other and even took on the University of Miami Hurricanes. Here, Louis Delgado, who arrived at BRAAF in 1946, shows his finest passing game. (BRHSM.)

Another popular sporting event at BRAAF was amateur boxing—both for viewing and for participating. Fighters trained in the base gymnasiums and fought in an outdoor arena on Monday nights. There were several weight classes. Ed Malavarca fought featherweight class and remained undefeated in 15 matches; here, he poses in a classic stance. (BRHSM.)

BRAAF boasted two movie theaters on its campus. One was near the entrance to the base, and after the war it became the theater for the Bibletown Christian resort. Here, eager soldiers wait in line for a ticket. Films for the week of September 1, 1943, included *So Proudly We Hail*, about the ANC, and *The Sky's the Limit*, a romantic comedy starring Fred Astaire and Joan Leslie. (USAFHRA.)

Svea Fisher, wife of Col. Frank F. Fisher Jr., hosted this farewell luncheon in honor of Mrs. Lawrence Carr, wife of the departing base commander, on November 25, 1942. Pictured here in the foreground are, from left to right, Catherine Ellis Wilkinson, Mrs. Frank F. Fisher, Jr., Mrs. Berkeley E. Nelson, Mrs. Lawrence Carr, Mrs. William A. Canterbury, Mrs. Charles W. Skeele, and Mrs. Ralph A. Palmer. (BRHSM.)

Herb Roth was a well-known illustrator and cartoonist featured in the *New York Herald Tribune* and other major publications. A seasonal resident of Delray Beach in the 1930s and 1940s, Roth penned amusing cartoons for the *Delray Beach News* on a regular basis. This Roth strip features Boca Raton Army Air Field soldiers enjoying a night on the town during the war. (Delray Beach Historical Society.)

The Guenthers and McNallys celebrate the Guenthers' wedding at Wert's, a favorite Palm Beach restaurant overlooking the Atlantic. The restaurant was originally located on the Palm Beach Pier. Lionel and Alma Wertheimer built a separate building in 1924 and named it Wert's. It was demolished during the 1928 hurricane but rebuilt, and by 1940, the venue had air-conditioning, then a novelty. One of its slogans was "It's better but it's still Werts." (HSPBC.)

Boca Raton's beautiful wide-open beach provided a much-needed respite for the soldiers at Boca Raton Army Air Field. If one could not catch a ride, it was a pleasant 1.5-mile walk from the main gates on Palmetto Park Road. Here, a group of BRAAF soldiers poses outside the Palmetto Park Pavilion on October 18, 1945; SSgt. Paul Schweisburg is second from the left. (BRHSM.)

In 1944, James Ponce (hugging palm tree) visited his sister, then living in Palm Beach, while recuperating from injuries suffered when his ship was sunk in the Leyte Gulf in the Philippines. After he was rescued by another ship, it too was destroyed the following day. He spent his leave at the beach with friends and in one of the 23 bars along Banyan Street in West Palm Beach. (HSPBC.)

Seven

THOSE WHO SERVED

Only 79,989 people lived in Palm Beach County in 1940; more than 1.3 million currently reside there. This phenomenal growth is due in no small part to the activities centered here during World War II. The Historical Society of Palm Beach County and the Boca Raton Historical Society Museum have been compiling the names and mementoes of those from Palm Beach County who served their country during the conflict in order to honor them and keep their stories alive for future generations. What follows is but a sampling of those stories.

In 1917, Curtis E. Chillingworth (1896–1955) graduated from the University of Florida and was admitted to practice law in the courts of Florida, the federal district courts, and the US Circuit Court of Appeals. Chillingworth enlisted with the Navy in November 1917. He served at both Key West and Annapolis, Maryland, and he was on convoy duty in the Atlantic on the USS *Minneapolis*. Chillingworth was commissioned as an ensign in 1918 and served until July 1919. After the war, he was elected as a county judge—the youngest circuit judge in Florida. In 1942, Chillingworth returned to active duty in the Navy as a lieutenant commander. He served at Jacksonville Naval Air Station and in England and Hawaii. He left active duty in November 1945, was awarded a citation for his service, and resumed his position on the circuit court. Chillingworth and his wife, Marjorie, disappeared on the night of June 15, 1955. Five years later, authorities were able to prove the Chillingworths had been victims of a murder conspiracy. (HSPBC.)

Longtime Boca Raton resident Dave Ashe (born in 1925) joined the Navy in 1942 and served aboard the tug USS *Topenbee* out of Pearl Harbor. Later, he returned to Boca Raton, where he became a community activist, city council member, and one of the founders of the Boca Raton Historical Society & Museum. Ashe (right) is pictured here posing with a friend at Pearl Harbor in November 1945. (BRHSM.)

Tom Kobayashi's family was one of many displaced from Boca Raton when their land was acquired by eminent domain for BRAAF; they eventually relocated to Fort Lauderdale. Although not interned, as Japanese Americans, the Kobayashis were forced to house a Coast Guardsman who kept a constant vigil on their activities. Despite this and other prejudicial treatment, Tom (born in 1927) fought for the right to join the US Army in 1946. (BRHSM.)

Legendary American sportsman Briggs S. Cunningham Jr. (1907–2003) was an America's Cup yachtsman, aviator, and auto racer who nearly won the Le Mans 24-hour race in the 1950s. He fielded and self-funded a private team running a series of unique Chrysler hemi-powered sports cars built in West Palm Beach, Florida, called Cunninghams. Briggs served in Coastal Patrol Base 3, Civil Air Patrol, hunting U-boats off Florida's east coast. (HSPBC.)

Jacob Murphee Boyd (1899–1985), a veteran of World War I and an avid aviator, was involved with the design and construction of the Lantana, Pahokee, and Morrison Field Airports. He served in the Florida Defense Force, Civil Air Patrol, and the US Navy in the Engineer Corps known as the Seabees. Captain Boyd received the Legion of Merit Medal and participated in campaigns in the Aleutians and the Philippines. (HSPBC.)

Heir to the Woolworth's fortune, James P. Donahue Jr. (1915–1966) lived in both New York and Palm Beach. At the beginning of World War II, Donahue served with the 1st Air Squadron, Florida Defense Force, and the Civil Air Patrol's Coastal Patrol 3, until he was inducted into the military in 1944. Donahue received the Air Medal in 1948 for serving in the CAP. (HSPBC.)

Willis Hitt (1897–1985) was a two-term mayor of West Palm Beach (1941–1942 and 1946–1947) and served as a city commissioner from 1939 to 1947. Hitt owned and operated the Pepsi-Cola Bottling Company in West Palm Beach until he retired in the 1960s. Hitt was commander of the Citizens Defense Corps and served in the Civil Air Patrol. He received the Air Medal in 1948 for his antisubmarine patrol service. (HSPBC.)

John Arthur Keil (1898–1965), a tourism public relations man, helped start the annual Sailfish Derby and brought the Philadelphia Athletics to West Palm Beach for spring training. Keil joined the 1st Air Squadron, FDF, as an officer and later served as a pilot, observer, and intelligence officer for the CAP Coastal Patrol No. 3. Keil received the Air Medal for meritorious achievement while participating in antisubmarine patrol missions between 1942 and 1943. (HSPBC.)

A 17-year Palm Beach County commissioner, John Prince (1892–1952) was instrumental in acquiring the land around Lake Osborne for a park. When World War II began, part of the land was taken to build Lantana Airport. Prince served in both the Florida Defense Force and the Civil Air Patrol. He had been a lieutenant in the US Army infantry and served in Europe during World War I. (HSPBC.)

Originally from Alabama, Capt. David McCampbell (1910–1996) moved with his family to West Palm Beach as a child. He graduated from the US Naval Academy in 1933. While serving as the commander of Air Group 15 on the aircraft carrier USS *Essex*, he was awarded the Medal of Honor by President Roosevelt for 34 confirmed aerial victories against the Japanese, becoming the Navy's top ace. On June 19, 1944, at the Battle of the Philippine Sea, his air group destroyed an enemy force of 80 Japanese aircraft; McCampbell shot down seven. During the Battle of Leyte Gulf, McCampbell, assisted by one plane, audaciously attacked a formation of 60 Japanese aircraft. He personally destroyed nine planes. The other enemy aircraft retreated. McCampbell's other awards include the Navy Cross, Silver Star Medal, Legion of Merit, and the Distinguished Flying Cross. He retired in 1964 and lived in Lake Worth, Florida. (FSA.)

Richard P. Robbins (1893–1966) served as a county judge from 1924 to 1961 and as attorney for the Town of Palm Beach. Robbins served in the US Navy as a pilot during World War I, and in World War II, he served with the 1st Air Squadron, FDF, and the Civil Air Patrol. In 1943, Major Robbins was appointed commander of the Florida CAP Wing. (HSPBC.)

Charles Weeks Jr. (1919–2008) learned to fly at Morrison Field under President Roosevelt's aviation expansion program. He joined the 1st Air Squadron, FDF, and the CAP at West Palm Beach, receiving the Air Medal for his service. Weeks enlisted in the Army Air Corps, made 16 flights across the Atlantic Ocean, and served in the American, European, and Pacific theaters of war. From June 1940 to 1991, Weeks flew 15,000 hours. (HSPBC.)

Anne E'del Deacon Fenyvessy (1903–2006) served as a counterintelligence officer in the Navy during World War II. In 1939, she received her law degree from Temple University, the only woman in a class of 45. After the war, she studied art at the Norton Art Institute but returned to law in 1952. Appointed in 1956 as Lantana's municipal court judge, she became Palm Beach County's first female judge. (HSPBC.)

Florida native John Carves (1921–1943) joined the Army Air Corps and earned his wings in June 1943. Sent to New Guinea as a B-25 pilot with the 71st Bomber Squadron, 38th Bomber Group, 2nd Lieutenant Carves was shot and killed by a tracer bullet during a bombing mission on December 20, 1943. He received the Purple Heart and the Silver Star Medal posthumously. (HSPBC.)

In 1942, Owen H. Gassaway Jr. (1924–2007) worked as an aircraft mechanic at Lantana Flying Service, and he was an unofficial mechanic working on the aircraft of Coastal Patrol 3. He enlisted in the Army and was assigned to the 565th Heavy Maintenance Tank Company and served in Patton's Third Army in Europe. In 2008, the Lantana Airport was renamed the Owen H. Gassaway Jr. Airfield in his honor. (HSPBC.)

Wiley Reynolds Jr. (1917–2005), on the radio, was born in New York. His father, Wiley Sr., was a banker in Palm Beach. After graduating from Yale University, Reynolds worked at the First National Bank of Palm Beach. He later joined the Florida Defense Force and the Civil Air Patrol. In 1943, he enlisted in the Army Air Corps, serving until discharged in 1945. After the war, Reynolds returned to banking. (HSPBC.)

Lt. Donald Ross (d. 1944) became Lake Park's first casualty of the war. Ross was serving with the 191st Tank Battalion in Germany when his unit crossed an antitank barrier under enemy fire, and he was killed by a mortar. A memorial to Ross and another local resident killed in action, Ellison Wilson, was erected to honor their sacrifice. It is at the intersection of the two roads named after them. (HSPBC.)

In 1943, West Palm Beach native Richard Brown (1920–2001) married Mary "May" Holmes in Belfast, Ireland. Considered 4-F by the military, Brown, whose family owned Brown's Moving and Storage, knew how to drive trucks. As a civilian working for a special unit, he served the war effort by delivering goods in Belfast, where he met May. After the war, they returned to Florida, where they raised four children. (HSPBC.)

Assigned to the field artillery of the 1st Infantry Division, Lt. Joe Farish (1921–2010) served in North Africa, Sicily, and England, where he trained for the invasion of Northern Europe. On D-day, he landed on Easy Red Omaha Beach, for which he later received the Bronze Star Medal. Farish participated in the Battle of the Bulge and met the Russian army in Czechoslovakia in May 1945. (HSPBC.)

Roy S. Rood (1918–2011) was born in Rood, Florida. After graduating from Jupiter High School, Rood took outdoor jobs until the beginning of World War II, when he joined the Navy. Roy served in Virginia; Jacksonville, Florida; and in the Pacific as an aircraft mechanic on the aircraft carrier USS *Hollandia*, which took part in the battle for Okinawa. Later, he returned to Jupiter and founded the multimillion-dollar Rood Landscaping. (HSPBC.)

From Chicago, Harvard graduates Charles (1885–1981), Gurnee (1887–1960), and Ector Munn (1891–1993) made Palm Beach their winter home. From a very wealthy family, Charles and Gurnee founded and invested in several companies throughout their adulthoods. One of those was the American Totalisator Co. (AmTote). Charles became the first president and later chairman of the board and Gurnee the vice president. In the 1940s, they invested in the Eckert-Mauchley Computer Corporation, which developed the Univac computer, the first general purpose computer in the world. During World War I, Charles served as an officer in the Navy, Gurnee enlisted as a lieutenant in the Army, and Ector served in an Army aviation squadron. During World War II, the three were members of the Coastal Patrol 3, CAP, flying antisubmarine patrols. Late in the war, in some capacity, Ector was engaged in intelligence gathering in France for the Supreme Headquarters Allied Expeditionary Force. One of his investigations was about the June 1944 Oradour massacre. Charles (left) and Gurnee are pictured here at Hialeah Race Track. (HSPBC.)

As a child, David R. Thompson (1921–2007) delivered newspapers and telegrams to many of the residences in Palm Beach. Thompson became interested in aviation as a boy and wanted to be a pilot like his older brother. After working with the CAP, he joined the Army and served in Europe in General Patton's Third Army. Thompson survived the Battle of the Bulge and was in Paris on V-E day. (HSPBC.)

Former chief of pediatrics at Good Samaritan Hospital C. Jennings Derrick (1907–2000) practiced medicine in West Palm Beach for more than 40 years. During World War II, he served with a mobile army surgical hospital in the Pacific theater and received the Bronze Star Medal with Oak Leaf Clusters and the Purple Heart. After the war, he returned to pediatrics, caring for 50,000 children, including several Kennedy children, during his career. (HSPBC.)

Robert L. Mosley's famous brother Zack taught him how to fly. Robert (born in 1923) served in the CAP and then joined the Army Air Corps, flying combat missions in the South Pacific. As a pilot in the US Air Force, Mosley flew combat missions during the Korean and Vietnam Wars. When he retired in 1973, he had flown 13,000 hours, 182 combat missions in three wars, and six years as a test pilot. (HSPBC.)

Vince Nelson (1908–1968), a local legend and conservationist, was known as "Trapper" Nelson. He lived along the Loxahatchee River and had built a camp with a zoo that was frequented by locals and visitors. He was drafted in 1942, went to basic training in Texas, and then was stationed at Camp Murphy (adjacent to his camp) as military police. He died under mysterious circumstances at his camp in 1968. (HSPBC.)

George Greenberg (1915–2007) worked in his father's Pioneer Hardware store from the age of 16, but he took time for college and law school. That education served him well during the war, when he was assigned to an Army research unit in Virginia. Greenberg was involved in developing synthetic coffee and a neoprene synthetic rubber replacement for leather. He eventually took over the reins of Pioneer Linens. (HSPBC.)

West Palm Beach resident Lt. Harry Grosser Jr. (1920–2005) joined the Army Air Corps in 1943. He was stationed in Italy, where he flew a B-24 Liberator on long-range bombing missions in Germany. During a raid on Blechhammer, Germany, his B-24 was seriously damaged from intensive flak. Flying alone and without escort, he was able to nurse his aircraft back to base. Grosser was awarded the Distinguished Flying Cross. (HSPBC.)

William A. Gill (left), Lillian Hortense Gill Mize, and her husband, William Paul Mize, seen here at the train station in Delray Beach, all served in World War II. Gill underwent training as an Army infantry officer in 1943. Lillian Mize served on the home front, rolling bandages for the Red Cross and knitting socks and sweaters, and she also worked for the Civilian Defense Force, watching for U-boats and enemy aircraft from the top of the Seacrest Hotel on State Road A1A in Delray Beach. After the war, she taught kindergarten but eventually retired from SunTrust Bank as a vice president. Paul Mize enlisted in the Army in June 1943, serving in infantry regiments and with antiaircraft artillery battalions, eventually becoming a sergeant. Before and after the war, he worked as a manager for the Delray Theater but joined the Delray Beach Police Department as the chief dispatcher. He also was the clerk of the Delray Beach Municipal Court. (HSPBC.)

More than 3,000 Palm Beach County men and women joined the armed forces during World War II. The City of Pahokee proudly posted a large sign listing all the residents from the city who joined the military during the war. As names were added to the list, it just started over again alphabetically—therefore, it is necessary to check through the entire list to find loved ones. The City of West Palm Beach created a poster after the war listing over 2,114 men and women who had served in the military. The Historical Society of Palm Beach County also combed through the *Palm Beach Post* and *Post Times*, the largest local newspapers, for the names of those who served. Those morning and evening papers would mention when a local was transferred, visited home, or was killed. (HSPBC.)

About the Organizations

The Boca Raton Historical Society & Museum is a nonprofit membership organization founded in 1972 with a mission to collect, preserve, and share artifacts and information about Boca Raton's history and serve as an advocate for historic preservation. It is the steward of two historic properties—the Boca Raton Florida East Coast Railway Station (1930) and Boca Raton Town Hall (1927), home to the Boca Raton History Museum. The Railway Station is home to the Boca Express Train Museum, featuring a locomotive and caboose and two restored 1947 streamline rail cars. The society offers a wide variety of entertaining and educational programming, tours, and exhibitions for children and adults. Our website, www.bocahistory.org, provides an ever-growing collection of online resources on the history of greater Boca Raton.

The Historical Society of Palm Beach County is a nonprofit organization founded in 1937 to collect, preserve, and share the history of Palm Beach County. The society operates and maintains the Richard and Pat Johnson Palm Beach County History Museum, an admission-free institution located in the 1916 historic courthouse in downtown West Palm Beach, Florida. Since opening in 2008, the countywide history museum has enriched the lives of children and adult visitors by making local history accessible, interesting, and meaningful. The society hosts www.pbchistoryonline.org, a searchable website that shares aspects of community history online. All of this work is grounded in the society's extensive archival collection of Palm Beach County history, which contains over three million donated artifacts and is open to the public for research.

Discover Thousands of Local History Books Featuring Millions of Vintage Images

Arcadia Publishing, the leading local history publisher in the United States, is committed to making history accessible and meaningful through publishing books that celebrate and preserve the heritage of America's people and places.

Find more books like this at
www.arcadiapublishing.com

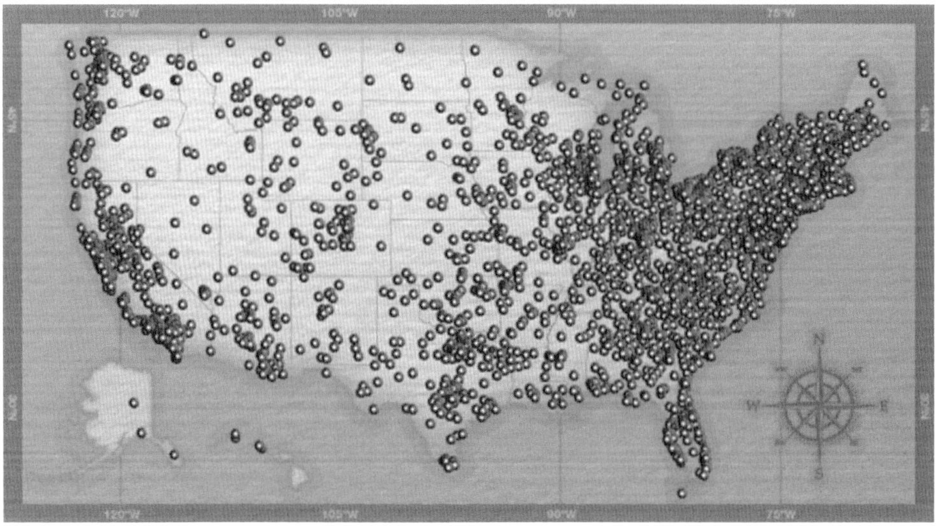

Search for your hometown history, your old stomping grounds, and even your favorite sports team.

Consistent with our mission to preserve history on a local level, this book was printed in South Carolina on American-made paper and manufactured entirely in the United States. Products carrying the accredited Forest Stewardship Council (FSC) label are printed on 100 percent FSC-certified paper.

MADE IN THE USA